New LEAVES FROM A MADEIRA GARDEN

Tony Powell

HAWKSMOOR
PUBLISHING

First published 2022 by Hawksmoor Publishing

Kemp House, 152-160 City Rd, London, EC1V 2NX

www.hawksmoorpublishing.com

ISBN: 978-1-914066-19-1

Tony Powell has asserted his right under the Copyright, Designs and Patents Act, 1988 to be identified as the author of this book.

Copyright 2022. All Rights Reserved. No part of this publication may be reproduced, stored in a retrieval system, or transmitted in any form or by any means, electronic, mechanical, photocopying, recording or otherwise, without the prior permission of the publisher.

Hawksmoor Publishing does not have any control over, or any responsibility for, any author or third-party websites mentioned in or on this publication.

A CIP catalogue record for this book is available from the British Library.

This book is sold subject to the condition that it shall not, by way of trade or otherwise, be lent, re-sold, hired out or otherwise circulated without the publisher's prior consent in any form of binding or cover other than that it which it is published and without a similar condition including this condition being imposed on the subsequent purchaser.

Front cover watercolour courtesy of José Luís Aguiar.

Dedication

Dedicated to my brother, Doug Powell, who read the early chapters but who sadly passed away before the work was completed.

Tony Powell

Tony was called to the Bar having graduated with an honours degree in law from the University of London. Most of his professional experience was gained in shipping and marine insurance.

Table of Contents

Preface i

The Idea 1

The Return 9

December. Funchal and its Gardens 19

January. Town and Country Delights 35

January. The Garden in Mid-Winter 49

February. Politics and Social Change 59

February. Land and Sea 73

February. Taxes – Monopolies – Poverty 87

March. The Garden in Spring 99

March. Antiquities 111

March. The North Side 119

April. Holy-days and Holidays 131

April. Mountains and Islands 141

April. The Garden in its Glory 151

April. Departure 161

Preface

Researching and writing *New Leaves from a Madeira Garden* evolved quite slowly and over many, many winters. Whereas Charles Thomas-Stanford described his book *Leaves from a Madeira Garden* as a *"trivial story of an uneventful winter"*, the writing of *New Leaves* began simply as a casual holiday pursuit. Having acquired the original edition from a second-hand bookshop, it quickly became part of the holiday luggage. Unpacked and back in the familiar surroundings, I would frequently be found marking chunks of the original text and making my own present-day observations, simply for pleasure. When the holiday came to an end, the book and notes were filed away, not seeing the light of day until our next visit.

As the accompanying pile of notes increased, it was then that the idea of trying to shadow the original work began to take shape. The pace certainly quickened in the year we made a second visit, enabling us to experience a Madeiran Easter, along with a trip to the Desertas Islands. By then, I had come full circle, having experienced Madeira in the same months as the Thomas-Stanfords. Then the serious writing and editing began. With the Madeiran juices flowing more intensely through our veins, the length of our stays expanded, lasting several months rather than a few weeks.

One could never undertake such an exercise in isolation and there are many people who have helped me. My daughter Laura (who discovered the original book), her sister Sophie and my wife Alex need to be congratulated. They have each endured the many hours in which I have had my nose pressed hard in the old book, occasionally resurfacing briefly to read out the unedited extracts of notes just written and accompanying me on the many trips discovering the Island.

Sincere thanks also go to our good friends the Aguiar family. To Titânia Mendonça Aguiar (the first person outside of the family and the first Madeiran to read a final proof) and her husband Mário. They have introduced us to so many parts of their island home. To Mário's brother José Luís Aguiar for allowing me to use his watercolour of Funchal on the front cover. It has meant so much to have local support for this project and, of course, their genuine friendship.

I am also very grateful to the staff at Preston Manor (from 1st April 2020 managed by the Royal Pavilion & Museums Trust charity) in Brighton. The Manor was once the UK home of the Thomas-Stanfords and is a unique 'time capsule' museum, well worth a visit. They kindly made available to me some of the archive material covering the Thomas-Stanfords' time on Madeira, which proved both enlightening and useful research.

Finally, my thanks to Ian Howe for the time and care taken in the final proofread. It was a great source of encouragement that having read the text he felt he wanted to visit the island for himself. I hope it is a response which others will experience too so that more people will come to appreciate the beauty and charm of this idyllic and unique little island in the Atlantic.

TP, 2020

The Idea

Leaves from a Madeira Garden was first published in 1909. It received critical acclaim and secured a subsequent reprint. A little over a hundred years later, a copy of the book accompanied us on one of our frequent visits to Madeira. It was discovered on the dusty shelves of a second-hand bookshop a few days before beginning a three-week stay on the island. Despite its being written entirely about Madeira, there's just the slightly romantic possibility that we were instrumental in introducing page to place for the first time. There again, it could have been light reading on countless previous visits, the book itself by now just as capable of guiding us as the words from its pages. Not knowing its history is one of the delights in second ownership of any book.

Conjecture about the identity of previous owners, where they and the book had travelled and why, can occupy the mind and provide a limitless source of fuel for a fertile imagination. This copy of *Leaves from a Madeira Garden* gave few clues as to previous owners, save for a single, handwritten inscription, in pen and ink, on the flyleaf, which read, "*The Hon. M[rs] Campion with the author's compliments – 6 August 1909*".

Assuming the inscription is genuine (and I have no reason to suggest otherwise), the first owner had significant pedigree and standing, certainly greater than the present one. But why was the gift made? A birthday present, one might assume, would at least have offered some indication of the occasion. Had The Hon. Mrs Campion expressed an interest in visiting Madeira? Was the book written at her suggestion, and was its presentation a confirmation that the work had indeed been completed? Had she spent her childhood on the island, her father a wealthy merchant, and the book a reminder of what she had left behind, almost as a sentimental keepsake? Who knows? Does it matter? Not really, just more on which a fertile imagination might lightly 'muse'.

The Honourable Mrs Campion was Gertrude Brand, daughter of the Right Honourable Sir Henry Bouverie William Brand (speaker of the House of Commons at Westminster from 1872 to 1884). She was a prominent figure in West Sussex (from where the author of *Leaves from a Madeira Garden* also hailed). She became the wife of William Henry Campion, a distinguished military officer.

Gertrude was a prominent feminist, assertive of women's rights. She also played a form of women's club cricket in Sussex, so I immediately warmed to her. But were there any other clues linking her to Madeira? Certainly, she would have come from the sort of background where a regular annual 'escape' from England's winter chills would have been a distinct probability.

Research has revealed that Gertrude Campion replied a few days after receiving this book, thanking the author for the "lovely book" and confirming "it brings my mind back to Madeira and its beauty." Clearly, she was no stranger to the island. She was one of many to receive a copy of the book. The distinguished writer Rudyard Kipling, a family friend of the author who had visited him in Madeira in 1907, wrote to say that the book "tells me more about the Island than any work I've ever come across".

The author was Charles Thomas-Stanford, later to become the MP for Brighton in Sussex, and later still, made a Baronet in the 1929 New Year Honours List. He used the monogram C. T.-S. at the end of the book's preface and I will continue to follow the same style when referring to him. He managed an annual four-month stay on the island (certainly one of very many) during which he began to 'gather' the leaves which form the substance of his book.

This was also to be one of a series of similar consecutive winter breaks we were to take on the island over more than fifteen years. A four-month stay has, so far, not been an option. A single visit of about three months is currently our record. But having spent a not inconsiderable period here, it was felt less of an imposition to attempt to 'rake over' the leaves, to sift through the papery leaf mould and put a modern-day slant to some of the island's attributes, adding a little of what the twenty-first-century tourist is likely to find.

C. T.-S. begins his preface by describing Madeira as an

> *inconsiderable Island ... long a household word in Great Britain ... its genial climate is remembered in many families as having mitigated the sufferings of an invalid relation.*

"*Inconsiderable*" in 'world' terms it remains, tied commercially and politically to Portugal, but with a clear and singular identity (not to mention dialect) of its own making, and perhaps, like many other protectorates, harbouring the dream of ever-greater independence and self-governance.

As to a "*household word*" in Great Britain, its name is probably less familiar since the decline of Madeiran wine's popularity. The sweet malmsey, drunk copiously in earlier centuries by royalty and the well-to-do, suffered a decline in the late nineteenth century when the availability of consistent supplies of fresh drinking water, especially in London, became the norm. *Haydn's Dictionary of Dates*, 1911, also puts the decline (around 1852) down to a period when "*renowned vintages here have been almost totally ruined by the vine disease (oidium)*".

A "*genial climate*" there certainly is, although weather forecasters, on a day-to-day basis, have a thankless task. Frequently the weather appears to give out a clear signal of its intentions, but it is a brave Madeiran who leaves home without some sort of protection from a light shower in the winter season. Then there are days, such as today, where to look up at the sky suggests anything is possible; a little patch of blue, surrounded by light grey clouds, with darker, more threatening, steel-like precipitations out at sea or over the mountains. On such occasions, what to wear can be perplexing. It's safest to let matters take their course. Today, the weather gods have simply not made up their minds. Nothing ruled in, and nothing ruled out, everything perfectly relaxed; why should they be hurried into making any sort of decision just for the benefit of we tourists? All of which leaves us to make our own predictions, safe in the knowledge that whatever happens, unlike Britain in winter, a sudden cold snap is hardly ever expected. Variations in weather conditions are only ever slight. Your own guess of what to expect could be as accurate as any forecaster's.

Two hours later, and our balcony enjoys full sun. I, appropriately dressed for cloudy weather, quickly concede that shorts might have been the better option. Such is life on Madeira with these little variations in the weather, most especially in winter, a part of its teasing charm.

*

It is symptomatic of the age in which C. T.-S. wrote that such a book should have been written at all.

> Many books have been written in English about Madeira ... Most of these books are serious works, written by scientific men, and dealing with the climate, meteorology, the flora, and other natural features. Of the rest, many have been produced by casual visitors, who, on the strength of a stay of a few weeks and a perusal of previous authorities, have felt qualified to enlighten the public.

Leaves from a Madeira Garden, however, falls into neither of these categories. It was never any intention on his part to write a handbook of the island (the sort of thing today we might call a Tourist Guide). Instead, he confines himself to inconsequential things, *"irrelevant jottings on many subjects"*. In this lies the text's unique character and gives it extra appeal to the present-day traveller who may wonder how things have changed in a little over a century, while discovering the island for themselves.

Twenty-first-century life seems to have left so little time for idle pursuits. Everything today needs a purpose or goal; we live life fast, with food, communication, work and recreation all striving to provide an instant response. Time to 'idle', to 'jot', to reflect, to ponder, seems to have been assigned to the past, but I hope that in adding my own twenty-first-century leaves, a little of the spirit of 1909 will also have rubbed off.

Time in which to reflect, to think, to observe, to contemplate, to exist, solely for that purpose, is important, and its apparent demise must not be allowed to pass unnoticed. If in these pages I also approach the irrelevant or inconsequential, it should simply be assumed that the seeds of 1909 have found a less stony ground on which to flourish.

*

Leaves from a Madeira Garden is a book which has one objective: to write about Madeira, the place and its people and nothing else. C. T.-S. makes this quite clear from the outset when he sets out his intentions.

But to talk nothing but Madeira is my purpose on setting out.

His were the thoughts, and they always remain the observations of an outsider. No matter how many times one visits, whether for periods of four months (like C. T.-S.) or if one joins the hundreds of other British citizens permanently living here, I don't think anyone ever feels a true sense of 'belonging' to a place. In this, Madeira is no different to anywhere else in the world. The cultural ties that bind someone to where they were born or brought up can never, to my mind, be acquired temporarily.

In *'New' Leaves*, I have followed the same chapter order as in the original text, save for those felt to be no longer relevant. Before too many people look to cancel holiday bookings, it's worth recalling that according to the National Archives, the last riot in Madeira took place in 1826, so the chapter 'Plague and Riot' has been assigned to the history books! Any 'unrest' described by C. T.-S. in the early twentieth century appeared to centre on the discovery of some mystery illness and the isolation required by the authorities to prevent it taking hold on the island.

The nineteenth-century had dealt some seriously heavy blows to Madeira. Blights affecting the island's vines were disastrous for the people and the economy: a failure of the staple potato crop; large-scale migration to escape poverty and near starvation; a civil war in the US bringing exports to this important market to a stop; and the opening of the Suez Canal, which meant fewer ships calling at the island. The catalogue of misfortunes mounted, one on top of the other. We don't know when C. T.-S first came to Madeira, but one must assume it began at a time when the island was at a very low point in its history, all of which makes a contrast with the Madeira of today that much more revealing.

Although the extracts I have selected from the original text give a clear impression of how the island appeared to visitors at the start of the twentieth century, the idea of these 'new' leaves is not to give a historical narrative of its development over a century, but to look at the present, with an eye on the past. It is a 'read' designed to be a companion on a visit, or a resourceful reminder of a stay already made.

It goes without saying that the Madeira familiar to C. T.-S. is very different today. One need only imagine how life has changed in

England over the same period. In place of water troughs for horse-drawn transport, we now have charging points for electric cars on our streets. Change of this sort is inevitable, as each new generation makes its mark. Nevertheless, to have a narrative of the past, with the vision of the present, gives a clearer appreciation of what might have been achieved, and lost.

*

A different style of writing is something which I am sure readers will readily appreciate. The language of the 1900s was far more expressive and descriptive than the brief utterances of the era of shortened 'tweets' or soundbites to which we are more accustomed today. The ability to linger over sentences; to savour the poetry of the language; to paint a verbal description with a full palette of prose; ample reminders of the use of semicolons; all are aspects of his writing which we are in danger of losing in the twenty-first century. I have quoted at length from the original text, to give the reader the chance to appreciate the contrast in style.

These quotations are all in italics, giving an easy transition between the early twentieth and twenty-first centuries. On occasions, one may question why I have included some passages (admittedly few) where C. T.-S. made slightly disparaging remarks. To me, they say much more about his generation and the lifestyle he led than they do of modern-day life in Madeira. Possibly not always 'pc', to me it serves to emphasise what Madeirans have achieved, and how far things have progressed over a relatively short period.

*

Do I have any qualms about disturbing the 'Leaves' that C. T.-S. so carefully laid down? I draw some encouragement from the fact that he was not averse to referring and quoting from accounts of earlier explorations of the island. He spent some time recalling the visit of J. C. Jeaffreson in 1676, while on his way to the West Indies. I see my 'new' leaves as another layer for the record, drawing attention to his observations, as well as reflecting upon a lifestyle of the English gentry which has now largely disappeared. And if, in another hundred years, someone was to set down more leaves, I would have few objections, quite the opposite.

In writing this book, the perspective concentrates on a glimpse of the past but always with the present-day firmly in focus. Visitors gain their own personal experiences, but it is also good to appreciate that things have evolved, as they always do. In being reminded of how things were, the reader will acquire a greater depth to their own experience of the island today.

*

The Madeira 'garden' described by C. T.-S. has, of course, several meanings. On the one hand, he frequently refers to the individual gardens created around the quintas, or country houses. He writes of uprooting banana, sugar cane and vines to create a garden; the wild and cultivated plants he attempted to grow with the assistance of local labour; the rockeries he tried to establish; the paths laid down, and always wondering how they were likely to fare when his current visit to the island came to an end.

Designed during the seventeenth, eighteenth and nineteenth centuries, many of these private gardens flourished, due in the main to a succession of largely English and Continental 'tourists' (of whom C. T.-S. was just one) who brought with them specimens from around the world to grow along with the indigenous plants native to the island. They quickly came to realise that the rich organic soil and mild climate meant that tropical and everyday plants could grow all year round. Blooms which in England might be persuaded into growth in a heated greenhouse, or cherished as small potted plants, might here flourish and become trees.

At the same time, the 'garden' reference was also intended to signify the 'garden' which **was** Funchal. It is in this latter context that the contrast becomes much harder to visualise. So much of the city is now urban, and the 'farms' which once accompanied the city's quintas have disappeared. Public spaces, such as the Municipal Gardens, Santa Catarina Park, the Botanical Gardens, the new waterfront and those wild areas in the city which have not been developed show glimpses of what must have been the 'gardens' of Funchal that C. T.-S. would have recognised.

These wild open spaces of the city, where flowers once flourished, have greatly reduced. Most private gardens have withered significantly in size too. Window boxes and tubs in quiet veranda corners are now the norm, while cultivation in private gardens on the outer limits of the city concentrates more on growing produce, which is understandable.

But I am in danger of treading ahead of myself. We must begin at the beginning and the point where the author returns once more to his winter retreat and the island to which he (and we) have become so attached.

The Return

By calling his first chapter 'The Return', C. T.-S. immediately dispels any illusions that his book was the product of a single visit. Although he first describes this book as a *"trivial story of an uneventful winter"*, he goes on to confide, *"it has been my good fortune to pass many winters in the island"*. His writing clearly draws on knowledge gained over many winters. How many of these occurred before he began to write is unknown. We know from later chapters that he was a visitor here in 1905 and 1907. On some occasions, he writes about staying not far from the village of São Martinho, a quarter of a mile from the sea, overlooking the Bay of Funchal, while on others, he describes renting a quinta at Monte. Voyage records show he continued to be a passenger on-board ships bound for Madeira for many years after the book appeared in print.

So, immediately, we realise that our literary 'travelling companion' was someone from an earlier generation, able to commit to spending a large part of the year away from home. Someone with a settled income, and the luxury of not requiring a constant presence in any one location to manage affairs.

I encountered this sort of lifestyle when newly married. Our first home was the gate-lodge to a country house. As I recall, we paid little more than a peppercorn rent, and as we were both still studying, this was especially welcome. The lodge sat impressively at the main entrance to the house, surrounded by woodlands and open pasture. The estate's park even had its own cricket field with a delightful 'old world' wooden pavilion, the floors of which bore the bruises of hundreds of metal studs from countless generations of cricketers' boots.

The lodge was discreetly hidden out of sight of the main house at the end of a long drive, shielded by an avenue of fir trees. For the elderly occupant of the house, tenants in the gate-lodge provided an element of security, a light at the end of the drive over winter.

Built originally for residential staff, the lodge's exterior was in keeping with the acres of parkland in which it stood, full of character and charm. The owner of the estate was an elderly lady born, I would imagine, not long after C. T.-S. She openly admitted that following her marriage, they had never spent a winter in the UK, nor experienced what C. T.-S. described as *"the blast of the Northern winters"* or *"London in the grip of freezing fog"*. They belonged to a generation able to avoid winters altogether. Instead, they retreated to some exotic clime, escaping the interminably long, dark winter evenings and the dreary sun-reluctant months, where daylight hours are cut short, served up in meagre, watery and impoverished rations.

*

As previously mentioned, *Leaves from a Madeira Garden* was not the product of casual observations on a first visit. This was not the story of a first voyage of discovery, but more a return to the familiar.

> *The return has ever been a moving incident ... If to youth the joy of the first visit with its smack of discovery and exploration is more intense, to the mature perhaps the sober pleasure of coming back to the well-known and the well-tried makes a stronger appeal. And if the return is an annual affair, if it is a matter of "flying, flying south" like the swallows, to elude the rigours of winter in the soft luxury of an Atlantic island, what it loses in excitement it yet may gain in a renewal of interest. As our steamer drifts slowly to her anchorage in the Bay of Funchal amid the pearly radiance of the Madeira morning, we enjoy an easy confidence that our short absence will have brought no startling change in a land of slow and little change.*

C. T.-S.'s departure for Madeira was aboard a packet steamer docked at Southampton.

> *Nowadays we are accustomed to leave Southampton in a boat of ten or twelve thousand tons on a Saturday evening, and to arrive here with more than the punctuality of most express trains at dawn on the following Wednesday; and we are disposed to grumble because even to achieve this our steamer does not put forth her full strength ...*

> *The foil of even a three or four days' voyage serves to enhance the beauty of the approach to Funchal. To that majority of mankind which regards the very name of the Bay of Biscay with apprehension, finds little to admire in the murk and monotony of the North Atlantic, and has too often suffered worse things than monotony in its passage, the hill-encircled bay with the town spreading outwards and upwards its varied lines of picturesque houses,*

and its wealth of sub-tropical greenery, seems verily an enchanted haven of rest and refreshment.

"Who would not turn him from the barren sea,

And rest his weary eyes on the green land, and thee?"

Madeira had been a regular port of call for seaborne travellers since the seventeenth century. In the nineteenth and twentieth centuries, the Union-Castle Line's regular mail service to South Africa found Madeira an ideal stop-off on the thirteen-day voyage from Southampton to the Cape. The service eventually became unprofitable and ceased operating in the late 1970s. Today, tourists arriving by sea are the sole province of the cruise ships, about which more later.

The first seaplane landed in Funchal in 1921, although they had no regular flying boat service until 1949. The airport on Madeira laid down a runway for the first time in 1964, beginning a new chapter for the island, and the start of tourism for the masses.

For anyone planning a stay on Madeira of more than a few hours, the jet aircraft and Madeira's airport is now the customary point of arrival. Air turbulence over the Bay of Biscay has largely replaced the rigours of the seaborne passage far below. In place of a voyage from the UK lasting a little over three days, we have substituted a flight taking a little over three hours.

For us modern-day travellers, the anticipation of arrival is short-lived. No sooner depart than arrive. No time to while away monotonous hours dreaming of the *"soft luxury of an Atlantic Island"*. I have always felt, like the Christmas festive season, anticipation can be as exciting as the main event. The fading light of Christmas Day afternoon seems to descend in double-quick time, while the collective early days of December hold considerably more hours to foster the anticipation, whatever one's age.

How does one prepare for a stay of four or five months, not just on Madeira, but anywhere in the world? To my mind, it takes stays of a month or more to transport the visit from being a holiday or vacation onto the level of residing or living in a place. To leave behind a former life, albeit briefly, substituting something else in its place, for four or five months, requires a quite different change in mindset.

With a two or three-week holiday, the moment of return is always within the mind's mathematical calculation. During the first week, the conclusion of the holiday is next week, and any thoughts of return are easily pushed to one side. When 'next week' does arrive, we may perhaps count down the days and only on the penultimate day do we cling like limpets to those last few, fleeting, precious moments. Too often, we find ourselves anxious to be doing, just for the sake of doing, to fill every available waking moment, not wishing to waste a second.

With a stay lasting four or five months, however, the return date is so far removed at the start as to be almost irrelevant. In its place falls a seemingly endless succession of days to be filled in whatever way one chooses. There is no requirement to 'do' something today. It's merely an option. And if you choose not to do something, other days are available. In this carefree state, the days just slip by. To lose a day due to the weather or for some other reason is never a day lost, merely one spent.

In the first month of a long stay, I have often experienced something akin to a form of intoxication, brought about by a surplus of days. It's almost as if the mind, in a confused, heady state, is constantly searching for an end date by which it may set its own timetable. There is one, of course, but it is so far ahead as to be almost meaningless. Modern minds cannot cope with such lengthy periods. We are too far gone, programmed to live in a series of 'boxed' short intervals, requiring a beginning, a middle and an end, and for all three to be measurable at any one time.

By the end of the first month, however, the number of days which have already passed just roll into one. You may even lose track of when you did something; you accept the next day in much the same way as a beach accepts the next incoming tide. It just happens. It is only in the last two or three weeks that the brain re-engages, registering that things are coming to an end, and so begins the countdown to the stay's conclusion.

The winter weather on Madeira lends itself well to longer stays. We have had many prolonged spells of hot, sun-drenched days, even in January. But it cannot be relied upon. We have known people visit for a week, experiencing a succession of incessantly rainy days, leaving them with a poor impression of the island's attributes. For those here for a prolonged period, the inclement days do not leave so much of a hole in the holiday calendar, as they would, say, in a fortnight's stay.

For C. T.-S., this transition to life on the island must have been much starker than today. Modern communications rarely allow one to be completely removed from life back home. I think he captured his state of mind succinctly when he wrote,

> *We are withdrawing ourselves for a season from the life of our own time and our own people ... We have passed completely from the conditions of modern social life as we know it ... life may be agreeable with much less fuss over its machinery than he is accustomed to make: that if unpleasant things must be done, the art of doing them pleasantly is worth cultivating; perhaps even – but this is heresy – that the habit of never doing today what you can put off till tomorrow has sometimes not only aesthetic but practical advantages.*

For C. T.-S. and his generation, much of the enhancement of the island's beauty was rekindled in those hours of reflection, during the days travelling, before arrival. Plans made of things to do and see; juxtaposing priorities; enabling him to arrive with a set of objectives firmly in place.

Arrival today is little more than a mere formality. Too often, the planning of a holiday and the anticipation of its approach become lost in a murky haze. The turmoil and drudgery of packing, with all the other arrangements to be made prior to departure, frequently combine to obscure the ultimate purpose. To have had three or four days with nothing more to do other than contemplate one's arrival, devoid of all distractions, must have been a delight. Those travellers could have expected to arrive in a perfectly relaxed state of mind, after a period of de-stress and unwinding, the like of which any yoga enthusiast must aspire to achieve.

The twenty-first-century holidaymaker, however, frequently finds themselves utterly exhausted by preparations for departure, with the impending moment becoming a time of foreboding, as if that great cloud loured above one's head, along with the inevitable question, "Will I be ready on time?"

How often have I **NOT** looked forward to going away? As the seconds tick ever closer towards the moment of departure, the appreciation of what has still to be settled can be quite daunting. Hence arrival, three hours later, at the place of destination leaves us in no fit state to do anything other than breathe a monumental sigh of relief – we made it!

Arriving in such a condition naturally requires a period of grace, perhaps three or four days, in which to unwind, before being ready to fully appreciate the new surroundings and to finally bury the pre-arrival baggage.

So, for all our increased speed of travel, what have we achieved? With C. T.-S., his three or four days' sea passage and our three or four days necessary to unwind clearly means we 'arrive' on unequal terms. The modern-day traveller may find that the first quarter of the holiday has passed before they are ready and able to relax and enjoy what they have come to find. Only then will they be in the mental state experienced by C. T.-S., being able to

> *reap some advantage in a more detached view of facts, policies, and tendencies, than if we were in the thick of the fray.*

Nevertheless, fresh from the *"thick of the fray"* we emerge at Madeira Airport, much less well prepared than our forefathers, possibly with much of the fray still firmly attached to our boots, but which we are more than eager to shed as quickly as humanly possible.

As an airport, Madeira's could be just about anywhere in the world. The first signs of life we encounter are the taxi drivers and car-hire companies, none of whom appear overexcited by our arrival. Unlike some airports, where porters and taxi touts clamour to take hold of your luggage at the earliest opportunity and to divert you away from the queues of licensed cabs, Madeira Airport has an altogether more genial and relaxed atmosphere.

There are assembled the usual clusters of family groups forming impromptu welcoming parties, each anxiously vying to be the first to catch sight of a returning relative. Then there are the banks of white name boards held aloft by casually dressed drivers. Unaware of the facial features of their next fare, their eyes scan every passenger's face, looking for the first sign of recognition or acknowledgement at the name written on their board. A few anxious tour guides may be busy checking luggage labels, trying to identify the next flock they must collect, corral and deliver to their respective hotels.

That apart, very little hassle of any kind awaits you at Madeira airport. More experienced 'arrivees' may have discovered the scheduled airport bus service into the centre of Funchal and will proceed on their journey unhindered.

> *Madeira is an island of volcanic origin, situate, not in the Mediterranean as some of my English friends suppose, but in the Atlantic, 600 miles S.W. of Gibraltar, and 360 miles from the African coast ... that it is about 35 miles long by 15 miles in width, of extremely mountainous and picturesque surface.*

> *The great mountain wall which for the last hour or two before our arrival we have been circumnavigating, the main range which runs from east to west of the island, is an effectual barrier against the northerly winds which prevail in winter.*

Our first glimpse of Funchal is from an altogether loftier perch, an eagle's vantage point. Emerging from one of the many motorway tunnels or rounding the summit of the neighbouring valley, the entire city of Funchal and its bay is suddenly revealed as if in miniature, spread out before us. One's eye is quickly drawn to the waterfront, and instinctively a headcount is made of the number of cruise vessels in port or at anchor in the bay.

After this scenic aperitif, the bus or taxi makes its slow descent, winding through the suburbs, to emerge near the fruit market and the promenade, well worn by our footprints from earlier visits. We are back, physically at least, ready to begin the process of unwinding.

As we have seen, this approach to Funchal is so very different from that of C. T.-S., who could have savoured his view of the city for several hours prior to laying anchor in Funchal Bay, described by T. M. Hughes in his verse *The Ocean Flower* as "*an amphitheatre of hills, swept sheltering upwards*". To this C. T.-S. added his own description:

We who know it well are aware that the coup d'œil from the sea, delightful as it is, reveals little of the more intimate beauties which await us. The houses rising one above another are foreshortened as we see them, and give no hint of the garden luxuriance in which many of them are embowered. We can trace the roads which fan-like ascend the hills from the town, but we cannot see the brilliant creepers and shrubs which here and there overhang the walls that line them – the Poinsettia, the Bignonia, the Plumbago, the Datura, which at this season must be in full flower. Yet even from the sea we can discern that the great mass of Bougainvillea which clothes with a raiment of purple the cliff below an ancient fort that dominates (or once dominated) the town is vigorous as ever, though not yet come to its full glory of colour. The hills above look almost flat in the brilliant morning light. But we know that their surface is broken into countless ridges and vales, which invite an exploration that is never finished; and that certain shoulders of rock are concealing from us grim ravines girdled with giant precipices. And, we know, too, that the peaks which enclose them are but the prelude to loftier peaks behind, and that beyond them again lies a very fairyland of beauty, the wild, forest-clad glens, the verdant and fertile lowlands, the awful sea-cliffs of the northern shore.

For anyone standing on the waterfront today, looking up towards the mountain peaks, the view is in stark contrast to that which would have faced C. T.-S. on his return. The backdrop of the mountain maintains its guard over the town like some high-collared winter cloak, wrapped snugly around the municipality's population. The hilltop crests point craggy fingers skywards. Frequently they may be capped in haze or low cloud and (occasionally) dusted in snow.

These clouds can be a discouraging sight to any first-time tourist, but one comes to realise that frequently the mountains alone wear a canopy. Cloud on the mountains does not necessarily signify a change in the weather, nor that Funchal will be similarly shaded.

On the hills surrounding Funchal, the *"ridges and vales"* of the lower slopes are much less obvious today, due to the construction that has taken place around them. Urbanisation seems to stretch continuously from the waterfront, right up to the village of Monte. Apart from a few tree-lined major thoroughfares, there are scant remains of the visible green spaces which would have been familiar to C. T.-S.

The church at Monte, of course, maintains its close watch over the town, although to the untrained eye one nowadays must take a moment to find its exact location. At night, the floodlit proscenium entrance makes this a much simpler task. Not nearly as dominating as the statue of Christ the Redeemer in Rio, it nevertheless holds a similar symbolic religious significance.

"Tracing the roads which fan-like ascend the hills", much like the church at Monte, is also best achieved from a distance by night. Street lights assist, picking out the main arteries of the fan, along with the interlocking transitory passageways, spread over the hillside like a giant spider's web.

In the immediate foreground, C. T.-S. would have been confronted with the chimneys from the sugar refiners belching out their defiance to the environmental gods to whom we now pay limited lip service. Very few of these remain. Some have been restored, and the chimney in the Santa Luzia Gardens is a good example, a reminder of a past industrial activity once pursued in earnest.

*

From out in the bay, the packet steamer, newly arrived from Great Britain, would quickly have found itself encircled by a plethora of small craft, their occupants all vying for the attention of the new arrivals.

> *And so amid the turmoil of arrival at a Southern port – the clamour of the diving boys, and the importunity of touts and traders – we return once more to our winter home ... this Lotos-land of the South, "plac'd far amid the melancholy main."*

Disembarkation for C. T.-S. would, most likely, have been via one of the ship's lighters, bringing him ashore at the pier affectionately referred to as the 'Entrance to the City', just down from the statue of the island's founder.

How often have we too taken a walk along this same pier in the first few hours of a stay on the island? To walk out to the furthest point and slowly turn to face the city and its guardian mountains. There can be few better places from which to view Funchal, especially at night, with its twinkling amber street lights. Like water on a parched sponge, we eagerly soak up the familiar view. We take no camera to photograph the scene, content to refresh the mental images stored in the mind's eye, in much the same way as C. T.-S. would have done.

With the island's familiar soil under our feet once more, like C. T.-S., we can feel nothing but contentment. We have returned.

> *It is but eight months since we left it, and our intervening experiences – the green lawns and immemorial elms of our Sussex homestead; those glorious nights by the Norwegian salmon-river; the routine of English life; the haste of travel on English roads; the bustle of Piccadilly and the pageant of the Boulevards – all these seem to fade into a dreamland of the past ...*

December. Funchal and its Gardens.

The villas which surround the town, and in many cases have now been swallowed up by it – Quintas is their local name – were originally country houses surrounded rather by small farms than gardens.

... the Quinta in which we live among our flowers ... faces south east, and looks across the bay to the rocky uninhabited islands known as the "Desertas" ... and across such portions of the city as are not hidden by the intervening ridges to the great hills beyond. Below us lies the little harbour behind the breakwater which terminates in the Loo Rock, crowned with its ancient fort; and farther off the roadstead in which the great liners ride at anchor. It would be difficult to find a fairer setting for a garden, a nobler combination of sea and mountain, with just the sufficient evidence of man's neighbourhood and handiwork to emphasize the natural grandeur of the scene.

Built between the seventeenth and nineteenth centuries, these quintas were originally owned by Portuguese aristocrats and wealthy merchants, including many from Britain.

The English Church in Funchal records that by 1822 the British population on the island was already around 700. By the late nineteenth century, some 300 to 400 people were choosing to ride out winters on Madeira. Many of these temporary residents rented quintas, either furnished or unfurnished, and could be regarded as some of the island's earliest tourists.

Quintas for rent were mostly to be found in the elevated foothills, and on the then fringes of the city. They could be quite rustic and individual in design, retaining the common objective of creating an integral union between house and garden. Town quintas and merchants' houses, on the other hand, were more impressive, and usually privately owned and occupied. They were more lavish, with accommodation for servants, even a private chapel provided for religious devotions.

Visitors requiring a quinta to rent would arrive by sea, perhaps staying a few nights within the city, while a suitable property was found, often with the assistance of an agent. The duration of stay and the amount of rent would then be agreed. More regular visitors (like C. T.-S.) would come to know what properties were available, returning to the same place year after year. We know that he eventually purchased a quinta in an area not far from the Reid's Palace hotel.

People came to Madeira for many reasons. Some, simply to escape the North European winters, and to enjoy horticultural activities, of which they were normally temporarily deprived. Scientists, artists and writers came to study, paint and write in the therapeutic and inspiring environment created, in part, by the tranquil surroundings of the country quintas they rented.

Many others, however, came for more specific reasons. The island's climate was well known for its convalescent qualities. Indeed, books were written just for this purpose giving specific advice on medical precautions during the sea passage; the efficacy of the climate for specific illnesses; and details of local doctors and chemists able to deal with and dispense medications.

For the quinta owner, rents provided a good return in income. Lettings were often for a long period, calculated 'per season', usually of between four to six months. James Johnson's book *Madeira, its Climate and Scenery* records that in 1885 there were approximately eighty-nine quintas available for rent in and around Funchal. The altitude of each was also recorded to enable visitors to appreciate the quality of the air to be expected. Rents for a winter season would have varied considerably depending on the type of property being let, the duration of the hire, and whether they were let furnished or unfurnished.

Rented quintas also provided an important source of local employment. Gardener labourers, superior cooks, plain cooks, waiters, house and table maids, stable boys, grooms and bearers would all be hired as necessary. Personal servants were sometimes brought from Britain, but the language barrier often meant that their usefulness was somewhat diminished. Local servants who could speak some English were valuable and could expect to be paid at a higher rate.

The proliferation of quintas around the city gave rise to Funchal being known affectionately as the 'City of Quintas'. The typical traditional quinta would have had a perimeter wall, with an ornate wrought-iron gated entrance, maybe even an impressive blue azulejo ceramic tiled lobby. A tree-lined shaded drive might then lead visitors through the gardens to the house, the house and garden sitting naturally alongside each other.

*

C. T.-S. would not be surprised to find that many of the quintas he knew, especially on the fringes of the then city, have been lost in Funchal's expansion. As for the surrounding *"small farms"* to which he refers, the land has long been put to urban residential purposes. It is difficult to look at the Funchal hillside now and imagine that farms once stood in place of today's white walls and terracotta rooftops.

By the 1930s, tourists' habits had changed. Hotels, rather than rented country houses, were what visitors demanded, and for much shorter periods. As a result, many of the once-popular quintas fell into decline. Some reverted back to permanent private residences. A few of the larger, more impressive ones were preserved as museums, giving a lasting reminder of the opulence and grandeur of previous residents, along with the manicured gardens which surrounded them. A few, especially those in the choicest locations, were converted into five-star luxury hotels and are the nearest one gets today to staying in a quinta. We will visit some of these surviving quintas in subsequent chapters.

*

Within central Funchal, anyone with a keen eye can easily spot some of the older properties which once belonged to wealthy merchants. We have learnt, when walking in any city, that it pays to stop and look up, rather than concentrate on ground level, whether this is to admire the architecture or to judge the quality of the building. Too often it's the ground floors which has suffered most in modernisation.

In Madeira, the first clues about a building's heritage may be found by looking at the rooftop eaves, especially in the older parts of the city. Three overlapping layers of tiles, one laid on top of the other, denotes a property originally built for an owner of the highest standing and wealth. Balconies are also more likely to be found at upper window level, with the additional eave tiles providing a little shelter for anyone on these balconies.

Two layers of eave tiles would suggest wealth of a lower status, and a mere single eave tile was for everyone else. The more well-to-do properties can also be seen to have small statuettes of birds, faces or animals adding a decorative flourish to the corners of the roof tiles.

Anyone deciding to undertake a closer survey of Funchal's city rooftops, however, should be aware that not everything is as it seems. More modern buildings may have adopted the same style, so beware of being taken in by occasional fake facades.

While rooftop gazing, another Madeiran architectural feature, which would also have been familiar to C. T.-S., is the tall, protruding watchtowers. Wealthy merchants would have had these built to create an elevated vantage point from which to scour the horizon, in eager anticipation of the arrival of some sea-tossed barque. In the days when safe arrival of any cargo was fortuitous rather than guaranteed, many hours would have been whiled away, gazing out from such a tower, waiting for the first sight of a long-awaited conclusion to a safe voyage.

*

With the quinta farms of Funchal most definitely a thing of the past, only limited vegetation is still visible today in the centre of Funchal. Mostly, it's the tops of established trees rather than open green spaces. In place of the farmsteads, the city has simply expanded with the compliant ease of an elasticated waistband, spawning hundreds of small residential areas.

> *The inhabitants have a positive mania for whitewash, with its pink and yellow varieties. They carry its use to the excess of plastering and washing all their garden walls, a practice which creates a dead level of uniformity and an unnecessary glare.*

Modern houses in Funchal still favour white, creams and pinks, along with terracotta roof tiles, providing a 'uniform' standard worn by almost all. They still present a level of uniformity of style which I don't find unpleasant. But Madeira is no Hong Kong. It has resisted the temptation to build high, despite the congestion. Low level is more the norm, adding a compact, aesthetic, almost village-like charm.

From a distance, houses largely appear indistinguishable on the hillside due to their density, with urban occupation stretching uninterrupted from shore to the indigenous forests above Monte.

Aside from the volume of housing, a familiar modernisation in architecture is becoming noticeable. The distinctive linear masonry-framed windows and doors (usually made from red or grey volcanic stones: *cantaria rija* and *cantaria mole*) are disappearing at a fast rate. To C. T.-S., such city houses would have been the norm.

> *The houses are irregular in construction; many of them, especially in the centre of the town, are of considerable antiquity; and though most are more or less modernized, some still retain their fine old stone doorways and wrought-iron balconies ...*
>
> *The Portuguese house to be in the mode must have the same number of windows each side of the central door, and they must be equi-distant. Bacon's dictum that houses are built to live in, not to be looked upon, wherefore let use be preferred before uniformity, finds no echo here.*

Some of the traditional houses *"in the mode"*, close to the city centre, are still there, although often derelict, awaiting redevelopment. Despite being in a dilapidated condition, their stout, proud facades refuse to acknowledge any sort of decline, even though, in many cases, all that remains is a front wall. Cracks between the boarded-up doorways and window frames reveal an uninterrupted view of the sky.

Those areas already redeveloped show the modern trend towards ever more glass and prefabricated panels, but, with each new structure, a little of the city's past character becomes diluted and possibly lost forever. Convenience in construction and the cost implications weigh as heavy here as anywhere else.

The city has expanded, not just up the mountain towards Monte, but most especially westwards.

> *At the back of our house a steep road leads to the district of S. Martinho – a village two or three miles to the west of Funchal. You mount very quickly,*

> *and at an elevation of about seven hundred feet come upon a pleasant road which is almost level for two or three miles, and bending northwards and eastwards presents a continually varied and charming series of views of the town lying in the great basin below.*

Today, a walk between Funchal and the *"village"* of São Martinho would leave you hardly knowing when you were passing from one to the other; urban development has fused them with a single bond. Funchal's hotel district is primarily located on this elevated plateau, with the *"steep road"* a regular challenge for holidaymakers keen to explore the old town while declining the assistance of the local bus service.

In twenty-first-century Funchal, cars and buses feature as dominantly as they do in any major city, in part due perhaps to the absence of any kind of rail or tramway. Consequently, parking spaces are at an absolute premium, with an underground car park, usually built for residents, seemingly a condition of any new development. The six-storey apartment building in which we have invariably stayed has four underground levels for car parking available. If one counts these, perhaps there are high-rise buildings here too; it's just that forty per cent is hidden below ground.

All this is in marked contrast to transport at the time C. T.-S. would have visited the island.

> *One need never be in a hurry; for most things tomorrow will do as well as, or better than, today. And being accustomed to go about the town in a car on runners, not wheels, drawn by two oxen, one is inclined to resent the recent introduction of two or three motor cars, especially as the streets are narrow and twisted. As their operations are limited by the nature of the country to certain parts of the town, and a road along the coast about six miles in length, and as the cobble stones and ridged hills must be very trying to their tyres and machinery, there are reasonable grounds for hoping that they will not endure very long.*

A vain hope indeed, as there now seem to be almost as many cars as households. Hailing a yellow taxi or taking a bus has replaced the necessity for calling oxen-drawn *"cars on runners"* or a *"hammock slung from a pole"*. Roads have, however, improved considerably. Cast a glance up at the hillside, and no visitor can fail to notice the vast concrete bridges which span the ravines, providing a fast, modern highway system. Linked by a network of tunnels, the island's extremities are easily accessible by road. Madeirans often amusingly refer to their island as resembling Swiss cheese, such is the extent to which tunnelling has taken place.

Surprisingly, C. T.-S. had such a system of roadways within his contemplation, although not perhaps on the current scale.

> *Save in the town itself there is scarcely a bridge, and unless one is prepared to venture into the ravines by tortuous paths, and to cross the river by stepping stones, it is necessary in passing from one ridge to another to descend into the town and to ascend on the other side.*
>
> *It would not be very difficult, nor overwhelmingly costly, to make a fine drive around the mountain basin above the town, at an altitude of from 500 to 800 feet. To judge from the fragments of road which exist, some such scheme may have been at some time contemplated. The French would do it in a year or two; but to judge from the general rate of progress here, it will remain undone for centuries.*

How wrong he was and what a serious underestimation of local enterprise! There are now 140 kilometres of freeways, of a quality comparable with anywhere in Europe, linking the island in a tarmac embrace.

But we are in danger of moving too quickly out of the city of Funchal, to where we must immediately return.

> *There is indeed a certain old-world charm about the cobbled and grass-grown streets of Funchal ...*
>
> *Girls filling their pitchers at the fountain; carpenters, tinsmiths, and shoemakers plying their little trades in open shops beneath the dwelling houses; picturesque country-folk staring open-eyed and open-mouthed at what to them is the bustle and hubbub of a great city, and on festal days crowding to the cathedral; such are among the customary sights of the streets.*

Cobbled streets are still much in evidence, even in the centre of Funchal, fuelling the "*old world charm*". However, only a very few examples remain of the cobbled ridged streets. Looking more like a gently flowing brook, or an incoming tide lapping over a pebbled beach, they ease the ascent or descent like a gradual staircase. In the days of oxen-drawn transport, they must have made steep inclines much more manageable for the beast-driven *"cars on runners"*. One of the best illustrations of the ridged street is a small footbridge crossing over the ravine near to the marketplace, just inland from the Praça da Autonomia.

As to the *"open shops beneath the dwelling houses"*, examples are still to be found, mostly on the Rua de Santa Maria, running parallel to the seafront, close to the cable car station.

For centuries, this long, narrow street would have been the industrial hub of Funchal, with double doors opening out to expose the workshops beneath. They must have provided a very confined, almost claustrophobic workspace, but at least the daily commute time was minimal!

As one walks the length of this narrow street today, it's easy to imagine the range of sights, sounds and smells which would have greeted the eyes, ears and nostrils of passers-by from the carpenters, stonemasons, blacksmiths, cobblers, weavers and fishermen who once worked here.

The former homespun industries have nearly all gone, but they have at least been replaced. Artists have adopted the space, with some of the lower workshops converted to studios. It's arts rather than artisans that now flourish among the fashionable restaurants and cafés. In many instances, one can make out that the upper floors of these former workshops are now derelict or uninhabitable. Nevertheless, their adapted use creates an interesting and eye-catching spectacle for tourists, with each doorway's unique decoration giving insight into an artist's favourite medium.

The project of painting these doorways began in 2011 and is known as the Projecto artE pORtas abErtas (art of the open doors). Even when the studios and shops are closed, an outdoor art gallery of sorts remains, a boon for all the restaurateurs. A potential customer, pausing to look at the decorated doorway, is a distracted target, and an ideal candidate for unobtrusively promoting one's dish of the day. As well as the decorated door fronts, time spent spotting the distinctive old door knockers (a clenched fist, with a few simple variations in design) might provide a welcome alternative to those tired of roof-tile gazing!

*

Virtually every pavement in Funchal has retained the stereotypical flat black-and-white cobbled mosaics or upended black pebbles which are a feature of the Portuguese influence. In the tourist areas, they are more modern and highly decorated, often depicting historical scenes. This would have been so different to the large slabbed pavements more familiar to C. T.-S. from the streets of London.

> *The public roads are paved ... with large cobble-stones, or with chipped blocks of quarried rock ... Hundreds of miles of country roads are so paved, representing in the aggregate an enormous amount of labour ... It is no wonder that the mason's trade is a very important one, and that the craftsmen exhibit a high pitch of efficiency.*

This paved mosaic 'art form', as elsewhere in Portugal, provides a smooth surface on which to walk, mostly devoid of cracks or unevenness. One would imagine that these almost delicate walkways would become slippery when wet, as they shine with the lustre of a well-polished floor; however, they are as fit for purpose as any other paved area. Madeirans must give thanks to an earlier generation who laid these unique sidewalks, at a time when manpower was both plentiful and cheap. Not that this skill has been lost.

Over time, we have watched these craftsmen exercise their skill in repairing or replacing quite large sections of paved walkways, which had been dug up to sink some new utility service. Sitting cross-legged on the floor, they seem to be divided between 'selectors' (those who fashion the stones) and 'placers' (those who bed the stones). Stones are laid close together, on a substantial bed of black volcanic silt dredged from the sea. There is rarely more than a few millimetres between each piece and because of the random jigsaw positioning, they have little room in which to move in any direction. A cement-like finish is applied to the top surface, which dries after a few days. Certainly, it's more pliable than large slabs would be, and without heavy frosts, salt, grit and other weathering materials, it endures as a tribute to the skill of the craftsmen.

*

Anyone walking the sea promenade beside the Avenida do Mar and looking inland cannot fail to notice one of the four great gullies leading from mountain top to seashore.

> *The town of Funchal ... owns four rivers ... In their lower course through the town they contain very little water, much having been carried off higher up by the levadas, or open canals, which supply water for domestic purposes, and to irrigate the fields ... But if heavy rains fall in the hills ... then their channels become roaring torrents, and the dirt they bring down will colour the sea for a long distance ... These rivers are separated by ridges with more or less precipitous sides, the buttresses of the great mountain mass to the north and east of the town, a range which culminates in peaks six thousand feet high.*

The welcome protection provided by these natural gorges, in evacuating water speedily out to sea during periods of excessive rain, when the channels of the levadas would be unable to cope, has been felt for many years. In 2010, however, they proved ineffective in protecting the town from loss of life and serious flooding. The town was preparing for Carnival week, little aware of the environmental disaster about to unfold. The flash floods and mudslides brought torrents down from the highest mountain tops, descending on the town like an unstoppable racing lava flow, all of which proved too much for these gullies to disperse naturally.

Drains burst and much of the lower part of Funchal was soon under a mass of water and debris. Forty-two people perished and over a hundred and twenty were injured in the hours following the calamity. Although the damage was not confined to Funchal, the important waterfront was devastated as water, mud, boulders and wreckage sought a natural escape to the sea. Meteorological calamities, however, are not a new phenomenon to this island.

Main flash-flood events in Madeira 1800–2010

Date	Location	Casualties
09/10/1803	Funchal	800–1000 casualties
06/03/1929	S. Vicente	40 casualties, 11 houses lost
30/12/1939	Madelena do Mar	4 casualties
21/09/1972	Santo Antonio	2 casualties
20/12/1977	C. do Lobos	2 casualties and 45 dislodged
23/01/1979	Various	14 casualties
29/10/1993	All the island	4 casualties. 4 missing, 306 dislodged, 27 injured.
05/03/2001	S. Vicente	4 casualties, 120 dislodged
22/12/2009	S. Vicente	Houses and road destroyed
20/02/2010	Funchal, Ribera B.	45 casualties, 6 missing

Source: *Natural Hazards and Earth System Sciences –*
The 20 February 2010 Madeira flash-floods: synoptic analysis and extreme rainfall assessment.

Rather than being overwhelmed by these sort of events, successive generations have had to deal with them, often using them to bring about major change. The whole of the modern waterfront was redesigned following the floods of 2010. The foundations of a section of the old sixteenth-century city wall were unearthed, and after careful excavation, a historical archaeological footprint can now be seen just below the marketplace at Praça da Autonomia.

Similarly, on the seaward side of the São Lourenço Palace, springs which had originally provided a source of fresh drinking water to the island's discoverers were unearthed, together with a cobbled street, all of which have now been fully restored.

As can be seen, events like those of 2010 were not new. The present-day marketplace, a focal point for most tourists keen to see flowers and local fruits on sale, was once the site of a hospital, with the Church of Santa Maria located close by. An earlier flood and landslide destroyed both. The church was eventually relocated further east along Rua de Santa Maria, and the current farmers' market built in place of the hospital. The original stone windows from the hospital found their way into the grounds of the Quinta Santa Cruz, where they remain today. This marketplace would have been a familiar landmark to C. T.-S., although open to the elements, because it was not covered over until the early 1940s.

Despite these infrequent meteorological calamities, overall, the climate on Madeira is extremely favourable, even in the winter months.

> *The range of temperature, whether daily or annual, is remarkably small ... The effect of this on plant life will be at once evident. It means that, putting aside questions of soil, and in a minor degree of wind, you can grow out of doors everything cultivated in a cool greenhouse in England, and some of the things commonly designated as stove-plants ...*
>
> *The soil is of volcanic origin, rich, dark, often reddish in colour, containing no lime. It becomes very sticky after rain; in dry weather it cakes and does not easily become converted into dust.*
>
> *I have appended to this chapter a list of trees, shrubs, and plants which we have observed to be in flower on Christmas Day this year in our own garden, which is situated about two hundred feet above the level of the sea, and about a quarter of a mile from it. It will perhaps surprise some that such a range of blossom may be met within mid-winter at a distance of eighty hours' steaming from our shores. Owing to the copious rains which have happily fallen during the autumn, everything this year is looking its best, and the growth of tree and shrub since last spring is surprising. At this season no floral feature of the island approaches in glory the Bignonia Venusta, the "Golden Shower". Of the most luxuriant growth, it is ramping everywhere over wall and pergola and trellis, and its leaves are almost hidden in the wealth of its orange flowers. Crimson Poinsettias, white Daturas, blue-grey Plumbago make a notable trio, magnificent in combination. Hedychium gardnerianum is over, but its orange seed-pods are a handsome feature. The great single Hibiscus bears aloft its fine red blossoms, individually a flower unsurpassed for symmetry and beauty. Irises are coming out; for the pretty lilac Fimbriata we must wait a little, but the white Stylosa, which I brought from England last year, is flowering already. Some of the roses are making a great show. Begonias of various kinds are in perfection ... A few stray sweet peas are in flower ... Comparable in colour effect even with the brighter flowers is the foliage of the Acalapha, with its bizarre combination of green and red and bronze and pink.*

So, even in the depths of a North European winter, there's still much to be found growing and blooming on Madeira.

The climate is also able to support four or five vegetable crops each year. Produce that in Britain we associate with a narrow growing season is pretty much assured throughout the year. Fresh runner beans on the menu for Christmas Day, something I would always willingly substitute for Brussels sprouts, are usually available.

The terraced plots on the outskirts of Funchal seem quite capable of producing crops throughout the year.

> *A square plot in front of the house, with a level surface secured by retaining walls, often on the hillsides of considerable height, and cut up into beds of rather fantastic shape ... level, or even undulating, ground is rare, and that the hillsides surrounding the town are, wherever possible, terraced. These terraces, upheld by rough or cemented stone walls, are devoted to the operations of the fazenda – the farm or vegetable garden.*

In C. T.-S.'s day, the fazenda would have been devoted to growing sugar cane, banana and vines. Although the vines do take their customary winter siesta, potatoes and other root crops are likely to be found, especially in the more sheltered areas, at any time.

*

It would be impossible to write about the month of December without more mention of Christmas. C. T.-S. is about to move on to January, welcoming in the New Year, in his sequential seasonal record. We must assume Christmas, at the time he observed, was purely a religious festival, without too many secular trappings. His chief contribution to the yuletide season was to list the different flowers in bloom in his garden.

Christmas or 'Natal' is a very special time in Madeira from both the religious and secular viewpoints, and never fails to please. As you might expect, the cathedral and churches are packed on Christmas Day, with standing room only. It is similar for the ceremonial arrival of the Kings, drawing the Christmas period to an end.

The coloured lights which seem to garland every tree and connect one side of the street to the other are literally everywhere, greatly adding to the occasion's festive charms. It is apt, for a 'garden' island, that it should be the trees and large shrubs around which most lights are hung. It was estimated that a total of 600,000 light bulbs were used in creating the seasonal effect in 2016, at a cost of 1.5 million Euros, giving an indication of the effort which goes into creating this magical effect. No two years are the same. Lights are taken down at the end of the season and the design is altered for the following year, which means that you rarely see the same arrangements two years in succession.

It is little wonder that tourists and locals stroll the festooned streets in central Funchal from dusk until late throughout December and into early January. It is best seen at night, when everyone immerses themselves in the uniquely created, family-centred atmosphere.

When did the tradition for such a lengthy period of seasonal illumination begin? The advent of electric street lighting would have been an essential forerunner. Perhaps it intensified with the realisation that Madeira's place in the world lay as a year-round holiday destination. Suffice it to say, a visit just to see the lights and hear the festive music is a reason for coming to Madeira all on its own.

In addition to the lights and displays, costumed Father Christmases stand on many street corners, adding yet more colour and seasonal atmosphere. They sell helium-filled balloons, in the shapes of animals or familiar cartoon characters, the clusters sometimes so big that their young customers have difficulty in deciding which to choose. Or perhaps their hesitation is in wondering what stops Santa and his charges from floating away up into the night sky.

Occasionally a forlorn stray balloon can be seen lodged in the upper branches of a jacaranda tree, waiting for a strong wind to complete the lone escape. One can only imagine the dismay of the young owner, who for a moment may have been distracted and forgotten their charge. The indignity of the loss is felt most keenly if it remains in sight, but tantalisingly out of reach. Tears are sometimes shed at both the indignity and the chastisement from those who, moments earlier, had handed over a few Euros for the future escapee.

*

By day, during Natal, the sound of music is everywhere, whether created by loudspeakers in lofty treetops or from the various selected vantage points where a stage may have been erected for choirs, bands and folk dancers to entertain, in rotation. Their session done, they move on to the next allotted staging post. Rarely is the music overdone or intrusive. It provides a wonderful backdrop, and a constant, gentle reminder of both season and occasion. Throw open a window during the day, and a breeze of yuletide entertainment comes wafting in.

> ... *the machête, a small guitar of four strings peculiar to the island, is often heard in the streets. In the country peasants frequently beguile the tedium of a journey with its strains; and on holidays bands of men, with perhaps half a dozen instruments and accompanied by an admiring throng, walking in step to the music, may often be met with ... It is "a measure full of state and ancientry", and the effect, if monotonous, is not unpleasant.*

C. T.-S. could equally have been describing these same bands of brightly clad folk singers and dancers appearing in Funchal throughout the year, to beguile and entertain tourists, as well as providing photo opportunities for hundreds of amateur lenses.

Occasionally, staged events are held in the Municipal Gardens and other venues around the city centre. Lack of proper seating can make staying for the entire evening, something of an ordeal. Those more accustomed to it seem to be less bothered, willing to sit on stone steps for a couple of hours, around the semicircular stage. Tourists may tolerate it for so long, before shuffling off for cosier cushioned pastures.

As nights can be a little chilly in December and January, a jacket or cardigan is often a necessary addition to the short sleeves worn by day. Around the outer edges of the arena, the usual collection of poncha stalls can be found, supplying this favourite alcoholic drink for the festive season. Sugar cane rum, mixed with a choice of tropical fruit juices, certainly spices things up nicely and has something of a 'draught excluder' quality to it too.

The evening of 23 December is a very special day in the Funchal calendar. Surrounded by all the Christmas lights, one huge, open-to-all street party takes place in and around the central covered farmers' market. For many, it is the start of Christmas proper. All, except those who must work, are there. While we may send Christmas cards to friends and family, the Madeirans prefer enjoying meeting up on the 23rd, sharing seasonal wishes and poncha, along with collective traditional singing and dancing. Many other towns have a similar market-based party night at Christmas, but Funchal's is the biggest of them all.

Christmas Day, on the other hand, is a much quieter time, a private, family-centred occasion, as it is just about anywhere else in the world. After Christmas Eve, streets which were bustling the previous night, fall strangely quiet. The cathedral doors, thrown wide open early on Christmas morning, are shut by midday and the streets deserted, save for groups of beleaguered tourists looking slightly unsure at finding themselves alone in the city. Even the late-opening supermarkets are permitted a brief, twenty-four-hour respite, although few will have experienced the heaving scrum of desperate last-minute food shoppers familiar from back home.

By evening, a few understanding restaurants may have chosen to open their doors for those tourists who have not entrusted festive mealtimes to a hotel's catering timetable, and who will have taken the precaution of booking in advance. And so Christmas Day comes and goes; only here, for us, there is one enormous seasonal bonus. We forego the unwanted early intervention of twilight by mid-afternoon. There are no 'light' rations here. Daylight, in December, lasts until about 7pm and is the best of seasonal gifts available to all.

January. Town and Country Delights.

The old year died in a blaze of glory. The passion of the Madeirans for fireworks, as pleasing not only to the eye, but to the ear, is extraordinary. During the past fortnight the Saturnalia have been celebrated with a continuous fusillade by day and night. Learned men will discourse to you of survivals of sun-worship and fire-worship. But these do not seem to account for the noise-worship in which the younger part of the population especially takes so active a part. The great delight of the small boys, abetted, it must be owned, by their small sisters, is to place some fulminating powder on a stone and to strike it just as you are passing, on foot or horseback ...

In the last hours of the thirty-first of December, the firework habit produces its fullest manifestations. The town, the suburbs, the country houses, and the surrounding hills are all ablaze with coloured lights, and, as the hour of midnight approaches, showers of rockets, of shells, of Roman candles, and whatnot rise in all directions. The climax is reached at midnight, when the rain of fire redoubles, the steamers in the port blow their hooters, bells are rung, and a most unholy din prevails. Then in a few minutes all is peace, save when some roysterers wake the echoes, or a belated bomb disturbs our slumbers.

This watch-night display of fireworks is indeed a splendid spectacle, its success being largely due to the hilly nature of its area, and its widespread extent. Though the individual fireworks may be of comparatively inferior quality, yet the whole far surpasses in glory set displays at exhibitions and such places, and the effect is much heightened by the fact that it is the result of private and spontaneous effort.

Madeirans have lost none of their appetite for pyrotechnics. The New Year, despite being in the winter season, attracts some of the largest groups of tourists in any year. The firework display ushering in the New Year is the centrepiece of the celebration. There are less of the individual, spontaneous and private displays these days, although once darkness falls, small pockets of backyard escapades can be seen taking place on the hills surrounding Funchal. They are the prelude to a central display that would rival anywhere, frequently seeking to establish the record for the largest, longest, loudest display in the world. While major capital cities wrestle to outdo one another, this tiny island hosts an event which would stand proudly alongside them. At its height, a ring of colour, sound and fury erupts, encircling the high mountaintops above Funchal and along the waterfront, watched by what appears to be most of the island's population.

It is not uncommon for a dozen cruise ships to be in port or at anchor in the bay, in eager anticipation of this great *feu d'artifice* to begin. On-board, New Year's Eve celebrations will be in full swing, but at the appointed hour, the moment is heralded by a cacophony from the entire orchestra of ships' horns, signalling the dawn of the New Year, and with it the cue for the fire play to begin.

The waterfront, or Avenida do Mar, temporarily turned into a pedestrian-only zone from early evening, becomes the venue for another giant street party. Young and old, families and friends, tourists and locals mix in the heady air of the drifting smoke plumes from the roast chestnut sellers; the homely, aromatic warmth of the garlic bread bakers; and the sugary sweet, fat-frying doughnut makers, who crown their wares in sucrose-saturated jams and sticky pastes; the poncha stalls, as ever, eager to entice one to try an innocently fruit-flavoured juice with its generous measure of sugar cane rum. It all goes into the mix, combining to establish a nasal symphony as varied and enchanting as the accompanying aerial display overhead.

Promenading takes place before and after the firework display; babes in arms and toddlers alike take a full part until, exhausted, they are carried back to awaiting cars and apartments. Even the occasional aftershock of "*some fulminating powder*", just discovered or held back for maximum effect, fails to wake them from their blissfully reviving sleep.

Those able to run the full course continue to promenade, socialising. How many romances are established or cemented in these fleeting hours, toasting the New Year with poncha or just taking in the Christmas lights? Attendance on New Year's Eve is almost obligatory, save for the housebound or sick, and few make their apologies.

By first light the next day, the younger, more energetic partygoers show little sign of tiring. By sunrise, all thoughts of sleep have been discarded. Instead, they sit red-eyed in the café bars along the Avenida do Mar, many still in evening dress, bodies desperate for sleep but with spirits unwilling to surrender.

Around them lie the remnants of what remains of a thoroughly good 'do'. Along most of the mile or so of the waterfront are to be found discarded streamers, party paraphernalia, bottles and thousands upon thousands of plastic flutes. Once brim-full of beer, brute, wine or poncha, they lie dispensed as liberally as the New Year wishes handed out the night before.

For the more sober onlookers, the scene is reminiscent of parents returning home after a night away, surveying the results of their offspring having hosted an impromptu party. On such occasions, parents might turn speechless and await an explanation. But in Madeira, an army of attendants will already have appeared, uniformed, well organised, working with purpose, to begin to clear up the mess and restore full order.

By 10am, as the congregations depart from their first religious devotions of the year, you could be excused for wondering what, if anything, had taken place the night before. Madeira knows the importance of tourists to the island and they protect and preserve their infrastructure as a parent might care for a newly born infant.

In addition to those tourists who may have travelled for a week or two, or longer, the island is rarely without its occasional drop-in visitors.

> *It [Madeira] is now the winter resort of many foreigners who are unable to find so equable and gracious a climate in Europe, and it is visited by an ever-increasing number of tourists, American, English, and German.*

> *From the United States especially come these invading hordes, conveyed in giant steamers of the White Star, the Hamburg-American and other lines. These vessels arrive with bands playing and flags flying in their temporary character of pleasure ships; and if ships have feelings, one may suppose them to be a little ashamed of their job. Their passengers, hundreds and hundreds at a time, descend on the town, buy thousands of postcards made in Germany, chaffer and haggle with the vendors of embroidery and wickerwork, which are local productions, and of various curiosities specially imported for their benefit; and lo! tomorrow they are gone – to invade Gibraltar and Naples, Cairo and Jerusalem, in similar fashion; and peace will reign until the next swarm appears. Of the real charm of the island these visitors see and learn nothing; of its flowery and scent-laden gardens, the wild grandeur of its mountain gorges, its hillsides aglow with broom and gorse, few can carry away any impression whatever ...*

> *But if this ignorance is their loss, it is our gain. These casual visitors touch but the fringe and leave the garment undefiled. Outside the limited range of their experience – the ascent by railway to the Mount Church; the "running-cars" in which they tobogganed down; the hotels where they raided the food of more regular guests; the Casino where they lost their money – outside these they know not Madeira, and Madeira knowns them not.*

It is not difficult to spot anyone who is "only here for a few hours"; however, rather than the *"hundreds and hundreds"* to which C. T.-S. referred, today one must substitute thousand upon thousand. The newest AIDA cruise ship, launched in 2018, has capacity for 6,000 passengers. Cunard flagship *Queen Mary 2* is said to occupy the same space alongside the quayside as forty-one London red double-decker buses!

Cooped up in their floating cubicle cabins, the chance to get ashore to stretch the legs is an option understandably few reject. After all, why else would they have come? If you are not going to step on foreign soil for a few hours, you might as well have stayed in a fancy hotel in Brighton and avoided the Bay of Biscay crossing. The gangway being lowered to a quayside must be a welcome sight almost wherever the ship is docked.

Sitting at one of the many waterfront coffee bars in Funchal in midmorning, watching the world go by, one's ear suddenly registers that everyone has adopted a German, French or American accent. A glance across to the port will account for the sudden change in language. A cruise ship will have slipped into harbour in the dead of night, and after breakfast its human cargo will begin the daily procession to and from ship to town, returning for afternoon tea and an early evening departure, in a seemingly never-ending cycle of port-to-port 'house calls'.

C. T.-S.'s conclusion as to the limited experiences these essential and valuable temporary tourists acquire in such a few hours is easily understood. Can anyone really say they know a place from such a brief visit? A few perfunctory hours on an open-top bus; or a wander around the flower market, and a hurriedly scribbled postcard etched out on the corner of some coffee bar table, is about all that might be expected. I would imagine most cruise passengers would return to their temporary floating mobile homes having done little more than rub shoulders with Madeirans. At its best, a brief visit to the island may just encourage a longer stay on a subsequent occasion.

One of the most enjoyable times for me during any stay on the island is to wake up, look across to the port, and see an absence of cruise ships. This may seem a little selfish, even contrary, and certainly wholly against the interests of the Madeiran economy. It's just that I feel, on such occasions, for a few brief hours, Funchal breathes a huge sigh of relief, takes an imaginary deep breath, sits back and enjoys a little R&R.

Take this morning, for example. Nine a.m. and the tourist shops beside the CR7 hotel were not their usual bustling hive of activity. Postcard stands would normally have been moved from their temporary overnight 'lodgings' in-store, pushed back into full sunlight, to catch the eye of passing trade. Displays of sunhats, brightly coloured T-shirts and assorted umbrellas (especially when there's cloud over the mountains) would normally have been thrust centre stage again, with a shop assistant ready in the doorway to encourage customers to come inside. Today, even the shop assistants seemed to be questioning whether opening their doors on time was a necessary priority.

The nearby cafés, usually busy with staff hauling portable tables and chairs from a lock-up, ready for the first wave of cruise passengers, were quiet, the pavement denuded of its customary additional furnishings. In one café, the waiter had turned customer, a role reversal with which he looked entirely at ease, sipping coffee and occasionally glancing up at the morning's TV news briefing. It was the sort of life into which he could easily settle. There are times when a café without customers is a waiter's delight, save for the absence of gratuities.

A clutch of eager tourist 'guides' also usually dance attendance nearby, vying to be the first to buttonhole anyone appearing from the cruise ships and showing the slightest interest in a day's personalised sightseeing. Prices, duration and locations are reeled off at breakneck speed; a means of transport is pointed to; "Come, take a look and see" is the simple request. Hesitate for a second, and a clipboard, hitherto discreetly tucked under the arm, is thrust forward, displaying an assortment of photographs, a sort of brochure-cum-scenic expectation for the day's excursion.

I worry that they appear ever so slightly too eager for the average UK tourist, who may have only just stepped ashore. Mother may be impressed, but Dad's been caught like this before. He shows no inclination to stop. Mother, on the other hand, wants to get the most out of her few hours on the island. A mini chase then ensues, usually with Mum (for she it was who'd dallied) left holding the clipboard 'album', first calling, then endeavouring to catch up with Dad, followed by the tout (anxious to keep sight of his clipboard if nothing else). Buster Keaton or Charlie Chaplin could have drawn inspiration from the scenes.

Today, however, even the tourist 'guides' had sent their apologies. The awaiting taxis and the neat line of three-wheeled tuk-tuks were stood down. Time for the hoover, car wax and elbow grease to revive the gleam and lustre in preparation for the next influx.

Further along the promenade, nearer to the town, one encounters the yellow-and-red-attired bus tour guides. Multilingual, with an unnerving ability to instantly weigh up which language to offer first. They eagerly sing the praises of their open-top sightseeing transport; offering a flyer to anyone looking uncertain; ushering those convinced towards the next waiting bus: or simply giving a welcoming smile in the direction of anyone with whom they make eye contact.

They were there today, of course, perhaps not in the same numbers; some had chosen a different sort of rod for today's catch. Like the nearby parked buses, all were ready to do business, but this morning the guides found they even had time to study their smartphones. Sitting casually on the promenade wall, soaking in the early morning sunshine, it was all so unusually calm and relaxed.

Surely it is moments like these that the whole of Funchal cherishes. A time when Madeirans appear to get the island back to themselves, if only for a short while.

*

But not everyone arrives on the island for just a few hours. For those with several days or weeks, how will they fill their time? C. T.-S. painted a vivid picture of the favoured pastime of the early twentieth-century tourist.

> *The Casino is in full swing ... Its very modest subscription is naturally inadequate to keep up the house and gardens, or to pay for its excellent music, and its frequent balls and entertainments. The deficiency is very comfortably provided by the game of Roulette. Such games are, I understand, as illegal in Portugal as in England; but in this delightfully easy-going country it seems the business of no one to enforce an inconsiderate law, and if such a functionary exists he is easily convinced that it is best to leave things alone. It is not for us English to throw stones ... An old traveller once said to me, "I have been all over the world, and wherever I found gambling going on, there were Englishmen in the thick of it. And perhaps it may be remarked that the chief patrons of this excellent club are English. It is a great boon to many visitors.*

Having read this account of the Casino (which lasted for a full six pages and left no one in any doubt as to his attitude towards the gambling game), I felt the need to pay the place a visit myself. I knew the location would be different. At the start of the twentieth century, Quinta Vigia (beside the Santa Catarina Park) was at one time the home of the casino. One can easily imagine the dining room on the first floor being converted suitably for this purpose, and the veranda, with its spectacular view of the bay, offering an ideal place to forget one's losses and contemplate a future less well-off. At the time C. T.-S. was writing, the nearby Santa Catarina Park was a cemetery, fitting, one might think, if ever a bleaker outlook was contemplated.

The modern Casino hasn't moved too far. Greetings at the door were delivered by a footman, dressed in frock tails. The smoky atmosphere would probably not have been dissimilar to one hundred years ago, but one can imagine at the turn of the twentieth century there would have been more of a Club spirit in evidence; evening dress and ball gowns perhaps; together with the array of *"resourceless"* lost souls, mostly male, sharing the roulette and poker tables.

I fear C. T.-S. would have been equally unimpressed with the attributes of those frequenting the Casino today. He, at least, envisaged participants playing roulette may have devised some sort of rudimentary 'system'; admittedly likely to fail, but that some cognitive process could have been at work.

Today, banks of slot machines have muscled the three roulette tables away into semi-retirement in a quiet, inconspicuous corner. Life in the modern Casino requires very little effort on anyone's part. Not even the pulling of a lever, just endurance and the ability to sit opposite a high-definition screen, hour after hour, pushing a variety of buttons.

It's all such a solitary process. Even an opponent in a game of poker is a faceless machine. You're not even aware of how well or badly other 'punters' are doing. But isn't this so very modern? So much social interaction has been reduced to an entirely solitary exercise. Facebook, WhatsApp, Twitter, require no face-to-face contact. Whatever one's view of social media, for many it does at least mean there is contact of sorts. As a replacement for direct personal contact, it comes a poor second. The solitary interaction from the confines of one's own armchair is greatly inferior to a knock on the front door or an invitation to meet up to catch up.

What C. T.-S. would have made of the Casino's coloured flashing lights and chorus of orchestrated synthetic mechanical sounds, heralding win or lose, is not difficult to predict. Participants appear almost transfixed, zombie-like, as if unable to avert their eyes for more than a second from the screen. Did they even realise it merely offered more views of the same? Some study of the hypnotic qualities this sort of equipment induces could prove very useful in understanding its addictive qualities. Interestingly, the World Health Organization has raised awareness of the problem by listing gaming addiction as a mental health condition.

I have no doubt the restaurant and live cabaret would have greatly softened the bleakness of my short visit to Madeira's Casino. I guess, like C. T.-S., it just wasn't how I would choose to spend my time.

*

Entertainment, such as it was at the start of the twentieth century, must have been extremely limited. A visit to the Casino, tending the garden, exploring the great outdoors, were the only things about which C. T.-S. wrote at any length. One can perhaps appreciate something of the excitement felt at the spin of the wheel, but for the non-gambling tourists who once journeyed here, they must largely have had to make do with whatever forms of entertainment they brought with them.

So, a rubber of bridge and a good book were largely what they had to make do with, although even the number of books necessary for a four-month stay would certainly have resulted in excess baggage charges, in today's parlance. We know that C. T.-S. could always request more books to be sent.

> *Book-lovers will deplore the booklessness of the town – which does not boast a bookseller of any sort. A few English eighteenth-century calf-bound volumes occasionally appear at sales.*

> *... the authorities impose a tax on books imported in any considerable quantity, although they permit Messrs Hatchard to post us single volumes free of duty.*

Later in the twentieth century, the expatriate community created several private clubs, such as the British Country Club at Quinta Magnolia. For the most part, however, amusement was found for oneself, either in the garden, home or countryside.

C. T.-S. does make mention of croquet, archery and of young ladies "*deserting the tennis-lawns*"; and of the game of cricket being played at Camacha. At the time his book was written, C. T.-S. would have been between forty-five and fifty years old, so one can assume his active participation in sports may have been declining. His passion for fishing gets a brief mention during his stay, but only in the concluding chapter where he bemoans the missed opportunities.

In present-day Madeira, making time for physical exercise is taken seriously. Gym membership, cycle racing, road running, football, handball, skateboarding, canoeing, swimming or simply walking the promenade before or after work attract participants right across the age range. A weekly outdoor exercise class for what appears to be the 'over sixties' had good attendance on the promenade this year.

Are modern-day tourists better equipped to cope with entertaining themselves, I wonder? Sitting in the Municipal Park Gardens today, I noticed, were a couple, probably of retirement age. Each carried with them an entire library of reading matter, encased in a Kindle or similar handheld 'tablet'. They were not unlike hundreds of other holidaymakers, able to summon up books, puzzles and games, almost out of thin air. They were totally engrossed in their chosen biblio-tech world, soaking up the sun, enthralled or alarmed by whatever fictional characters they had invited to journey with them on their holiday.

Occasionally, one of them became distracted from the small screen, perhaps at a chapter's end, and having been brought out of their self-induced literary trance, made a brief comment to the other. The result was a collective glance at something of interest nearby, or perhaps it was the signal that one at least needed a break from bookish pursuits, to take refreshment in a nearby coffee bar.

A twenty-first-century café culture in the centre of Funchal is certainly in vogue. The Golden Gate Grand Café and the Ritz, both on Avenida Arriaga, would have been here at the time C. T.-S. visited, and were regular meeting points for tourists and prominent businesspeople alike. Today, they share the same allure along with hundreds of other venues, large and small, throughout the city.

> *Some will regret that there are no sandy dunes by the sea-shore whereon to essay the putting of a little ball into small holes "with instruments singularly ill-adapted to the purpose"; others the absence, or scarcity, of partridges. Some the want of roads suitable for motors and bicycles ...*
>
> *In the modern sense there is "nothing to do" – no golf, no motoring (to speak of), no sports of the field.*

For anyone wishing to try their hand at putting little balls into small holes, the previous absence of facilities has been completely rectified. The golf course at Santo da Serra is of a standard that merits inclusion in the European PGA Tour. The Club House has a spectacular panoramic view over the south-east corner of the island. A mountainous backdrop, with the main course apparently falling away to the sea, it's a location many would envy, and the equal of anywhere in the world. Even the Island of Porto Santo, which also prides itself in the ability to offer splendid golf, is visible on a good day, along with the rugged cliffs of the Ponta de São Lourenço peninsula and the Desertas Islands.

For anyone willing to take on the course, the biggest challenge is to disregard the illusion that, when driving off, the ball is likely to keep running down and over the cliff edge, into the largest water hazard of them all. The sea is a good distance away, and one must expect very tired legs on the back nine holes as you return from whence you came. With golf bags and trollies safely stowed in the car boot, the warmth and hospitality of the Club House will quickly revive aching limbs.

Closer to Funchal, the Quinta Palheiro golf course provides similarly spectacular views across Funchal Bay and the south-west coastal areas. Although it is slightly less mountainous, golf on Madeira is not for the faint-hearted.

*

For many holidaying on Madeira today, a stay would not be complete without a short walking excursion, and a levada walk is likely to be what's chosen. The levadas would, of course, have been as familiar to C. T.-S. as they are to present-day travellers.

> *Much of the finest scenery of Madeira is rendered accessible to the adventurous through the levadas, or channels, by which water is collected in the higher hills and brought down to irrigate the lower regions. They are commonly cut out of the rock, or built of masonry, on the steep hillsides, and the watercourse is usually protected by a parapet about eighteen inches wide. Their construction must often have presented great difficulties, it having been necessary in many cases to let down the workmen by ropes from above. As their existence is essential to the cultivation of the lower lands they are generally kept in good repair, and those who have steady heads, and dare to walk by so narrow a path along the face of giant precipices, may reach magnificent scenery otherwise unapproachable. As the levadas must of course follow every deviation of the hillside their length is often very great, and it may sometimes involve a walk of fifteen or twenty miles to reach a point not more than two or three miles distant in a straight line. Here and there it may be necessary to creep through tunnels, and perhaps to walk in the water channel itself; sometimes an overhanging rock will make the passage of the narrow parapet, with a thousand feet of precipice below, a rather blood-curdling business; but the reward is great. We are conducted into the very heart and penetralia of the mountain solitude, and may feast our eyes on ever-changing vistas of forest-clad cliffs and soaring crags.*

It is important, in introducing anyone to the Madeiran levadas, to point out the sometimes lonely, inhospitable and positively dangerous places they can be, and the section quoted above does that well. In planning any levada excursion of one's own, it is essential to ensure the levada walk is open and safe and what precautions are necessary. Closure of sections is not at all unusual with little warning.

Closest to Funchal, a levada heading in the direction of Camara de Lobos (the Levada dos Piornais) is easily accessible. Nor is it difficult to find, best picked up from just above the Maritimo football stadium to the west of Funchal, and on a good bus route.

Sometimes even this levada can be a little treacherous. Random paving slabs may be found to be missing. One should always remember to **stop** when taking in the view. It's too easy to risk failing to spot a missing paving slab and sustaining an avoidable injury.

This levada heads out above the hotel district, before entering banana plantations and more rural retreats. The attraction of walking this levada is that you are rarely too far from civilisation. When tiredness sets in, simply drop down to the nearest main road and wait for a bus back to Funchal.

Two other levadas close to Funchal, east of Monte (Levada dos Tornos and Levada da Serra – a levada leading to Camacha and Santo da Serra which we encounter again in a later chapter) are also usually accessible.

We have, however, made many excursions in search of more obscure levadas within reach of Funchal, which a tourist guidebook suggested were there, but which after several hours of weary searching we were forced to abandon or retrace our steps, usually because the levada disappeared into a long, unlit tunnel for which we were unprepared. It is always good to remember that the levadas were built for irrigation, not as tourist attractions. We have often also found that residents are none too familiar with their location either, nor why on earth anyone should want to find the more remote ones. A puzzled look often accompanies the response to the question, "Which way to the levada?" I guess it's a little like stopping someone on the Strand and asking them directions to the nearest main drain outlet.

Over time, we have certainly appreciated the considerable benefits of taking a guide. Group-led walks invariably mix nationalities as well as abilities, heading along safe terrain, suitable for anyone with a good set of walking shoes. Watering holes can be infrequent, although the experienced guide should steer you in the right direction at some stage. Just occasionally, you may also find a friendly local resident, keen to offer produce from their garden, and appearing at their garden gate with a selection of fruits, happy to hand them over for a small donation.

Guided levada walks vary in length and difficulty, but a visit to one of the many Tourist Offices should provide a wide selection plus some good advice on what to expect. We have always found the biggest bonus of led walks is being picked up and transported to and from the start point, by minibus or taxi, rather than trying to meet the requirements of local bus timetables. This, along with the guide's local knowledge, is to be much valued. The downside can be a feeling of lack of progress if the walk is stopped too frequently, whether it be to point out things of interest or just to allow slower walkers the chance to catch up. Nearly always, guided walks tend to progress at the speed of the slowest walker. These, however, are small issues when placed alongside the chance to meet new people, and they have very rarely disappointed.

Whether on a led walk or making one's own excursion, there are times when a good head for heights is needed and an ability to negotiate the narrowest of levada paths, no more than a foot wide, with sheer drops to one side. Reports of accidents, even fatalities, are not unheard of, so regard for one's personal safety must be given utmost priority.

*

C. T.-S. concludes his chapter 'January – Town and Country Delights' with a description of an afternoon excursion to Ribeiro Frio and the Vale de Ribeira da Metade. In the early twentieth century, such a journey would have been vastly different to the simple minibus tour enjoyed today. In joining him on this picnic, perhaps today's traveller will gain a fuller appreciation of the once wilderness in which they now tread, adding a different perspective to their own experience.

> *So on one of the earliest days of the year we start from the Mount for the Ribeiro Frio, "the Cold River", a stream running northwards from the main chain, near to which is a celebrated point of view, the spot chosen for our picnic. A dog and several horses, with their attendants, form our cavalcade ... We ascend rapidly through pine-woods, pausing where there is an opening to look back at the city lying below us ... When we emerge from the pine-woods, at an altitude of nearly four thousand feet, we enter a bleak moorland region with great heaths and bilberry bushes ... Our uphill journey ends at a shelter-hut on the top of the pass, where the northern ocean comes into view ... From the moor we reach the valley by a road of steep zigzags, in woods of laurel, with an undergrowth of fern. Through this forest glade ... meanders the Cold River. But this is not what we have come out*

to see. We leave our horses on its banks, ascend a slope of some two hundred feet to a levada, pass along it by a cutting through one of the narrow ridges characteristic of Madeira scenery, and in a few minutes are in the presence of one of the world's great views. Climbing onto an isolated rock we look down into the vast valley of the Metade, with its precipitous sides rising apparently sheer from its floor upwards some five thousand feet to the pinnacles of the highest mountains ... The valley is widest, and circular in form, at its head. Mysterious and only half-seen minor valleys branch from the main body, separated from each other by the buttresses of the mountain range. Far below us foams the torrent, a small stream itself, but dowered by the reverberations of a thousand echoes with the roar of a great river. High over all tower the masses of Ruivo and Arriero, and the inaccessible crags of the Torres which lie between them.

As filled with a delight not unmixed with awe, we linger in the presence of this majestic scene, scarcely touched and in no way spoilt by the hand of man.

January. The Garden in Mid-Winter.

What do Madeirans make of their temporary island guests, those of us who choose to spend more than just a few hours here in winter? It's surely a legitimate question, for we descend on the island in large numbers, like some straggly flock of birds in search of a warmer clime, blown off course from the more usual migrating routes. By and large, our arrival, now a familiar annual ritual, seems to attract very little attention. These days, the island has more than enough accommodation, no matter how long we plan to stay. New hotels seem to spring up regularly, so they are clearly pleased to take as many of us as are willing to make the winter journey out into the Atlantic.

Interestingly, C. T.-S. also entertained similar thoughts about what Madeirans made of him and his fellow quinta 'sitters'.

> *If our servants are to us a strange and interesting study, what must we be to them? We come heaven knows whence, not at the joyous season of the vintage, but when days are shortest and rains are cold; we profess an impious religion which will conduct us surely to damnation; our manners are odious — we don't even know how to take off our hats; we make a ridiculous fuss about boiled water and such trifles; our pockets are apparently overflowing with boundless wealth, and yet we make ourselves hot digging in the garden; we scour inhospitable mountains with no comprehensible object; we are always hunting for old and rickety chairs and tables, and paying for them at least the price of new ones; we exhibit and expect a most uncomfortable amount of energy, when there is really no necessity to hurry or to fuss; and just when the warmth of spring is flooding our gardens, which we profess to love, with the richest treasures, we are off again.*

During January, Madeirans will generally retreat indoors, preferring the cosiness of the coffee bar's interior. They wrap their more junior offspring in scarves and woolly hats, tugging them down over the ears to ward off some imaginary chill. We newly arrived northern cousins, on the other hand, think nothing of parading around in shorts and T-shirts as if we had something to prove in this most docile of climates. This disparity in our respective attitudes to the season is taken very much in their stride. They probably find us at best amusing, even if our behaviour is just a little bizarre.

As the world seems to have shrunk thanks to the ease of travel, most of us now conform to variations of the same lifestyle, so we perhaps appear less odd than we once were. Or maybe it's the passage of time and the frequency of our visits which has allowed Madeirans to grow accustomed to our slightly unorthodox behaviour.

There again, apart from hotel staff, shop assistants and taxi drivers, we have much less direct personal contact with Madeirans than C. T.-S would have done. He would have lived alongside them, mixing daily with a variety of staff employed at the quinta. A few of them are introduced to us.

> *Our first head gardener, Manoel, might with education have gone far; in middle life he had taught himself to read and write not only Portuguese but English ...*

> *[The] custom of regarding the foreign visitor as a milch cow is deeply ingrained in the servant class here. It is a consideration ever present to us in our dealings with our otherwise excellent cook, whose pleasant and profitable business it is to market for us. We hear dark rumours that he is buying house property in the town, and we have an uneasy feeling that if every one had his due, those houses would be ours ...*

> *We have now promoted an excellent youth who has been with us as an under-gardener for several years... He is overjoyed at his rise in the world, and for some days murmured "muito contente" whenever I went within a few yards of him. He is to get married on the strength of it ...*

> *These sturdy Portuguese countrymen ... are of great strength and endurance, and, if somewhat excitable, gifted with a certain doggedness ...*

> *The good manners which are so marked a characteristic of the Portuguese upper classes are shared by the lower. To their social superiors they are respectful without servility, and they are uniformly courteous to each other.*

*

Notwithstanding the winter season, many tourists will visit the island to take stock of the Madeiran gardens during the horticultural equivalent of the 'closed season'. I am sure most would benefit more from a viewing during April or May. Yet, even in January, they are to be found in the parks and gardens, earnestly looking for whatever might be in flower. Perhaps, because gardens at home are at their low point, with all memory of the previous summer's magnificence almost completely faded, it is now that they choose to visit Madeira, almost as if looking for some sign of reassurance.

Casting an eye over any English garden in midwinter, it can seem impossible to believe that from those decayed remnants and frozen, sodden clumps of earth, where not even a weed stakes a fresh claim to possession, new life will eventually return. It's as if the keen gardener needs to observe fresh growth, just to be convinced that the growing cycle will repeat itself once more.

Although not in its floral 'Sunday best', those doubting botanical Thomases will still find much to revive the spirit on Madeira. Even in the depths of winter, there are hints of floral displays unimaginable in the UK.

C. T.-S. clearly cherished the opportunity Madeira gave him to tend a garden all year round. In Madeira, he came across plants unheard of in England, despite an issue with somewhat dubious names.

> *In our Madeira gardens, rich with – "Flowers of all heaven and lovelier than their names" – we have so many plants not yet endowed with English titles, that we are driven perforce to the Botanical Dictionary ... I nurse – I positively dandle – an ever-lively grievance that the splendid flowering shrubs of the banana tribe are called by the awful name Strelitzia. What in the world is the Duchy doing in this galley? Latin generic names are not of necessity hideous or unfitting. Those which are based on some peculiarity of the plant or its habitat are the pleasantest; such as geranium "crane's bill"; arenaria "sandwort"; saxifraga "stone-breaker". Names derived from celebrated botanists, if often ugly, are perhaps not inappropriate ...*
>
> *A Society for the Protection of Flowers from being called Bad Names is one of the crying needs of the day. When the Board of Agriculture can spare*

> *time from the pursuit of gooseberry mildew it ought to take the matter up; but I fear that until a florist or two has been lynched nothing will be done.*

Despite the rather raw nerve which seems to have been touched here, even non-tillers of the soil can appreciate the splendour of the cultivated borders, and the delight of unexpectedly finding a cascading bush in bloom, even at this time of year. One doesn't necessarily need to know the name to appreciate the splendour. Horticultural beauty is visual and sensory, and there's much to admire here, even in January.

For C. T.-S., I believe the true joy of tending his own garden came in the viewing and especially in being able to share the delights with any visitors.

> *One of the pleasures of a garden is to show it to the appreciative visitor; and this is a pleasure which we very frequently enjoy here. New-comers usually express genuine astonishment at the floral luxuriance, and friends who land from passing steamers are of course prepared to enjoy anything.*

Some of this pleasure, I am sure, was derived from the part he had played in designing and creating the garden's landscape. In this chapter, C. T.-S., having been back on the island again for several weeks, and finding his horticultural instincts fully revived, takes us on a guided verbal tour of his garden.

> *... six years ago our house stood in the middle of several acres of banana trees, with a small garden plot in front. The whole property is on a moderate slope, facing to the south-east, and is divided into about half a dozen main terraces. We resisted the blandishments of those who would have us lay out a garden on a preconceived scheme. In succeeding years we have taken different pieces of ground from the fazenda, and turned them into flower garden; – here a little lawn with a belt of white datura on either side; there a walk bordered by cypresses, which serve as frames for exquisite views of sea and mountain; here a long pergola covered with roses ... there a little winding path, bordered with rosemary, among tall shrubs, the many hued Acalapha, and the giant Strelitzia with its strangely beaked blossom. This method of proceeding has had the advantage of giving us continued employment, and if we do not use up all our ground too quickly, may be continued almost indefinitely ... On either side of the entrance drive, which ascends in a curve from the gate to the level of the house, we cleared a broad belt in which palms rise from a carpet of geranium and pelargonium, and are already asserting their supremacy over lesser trees and shrubs. The iron*

> *railing which bounds this drive is no longer visible, being covered from end to end with the Chinese white single rose, not yet in flower, but in March to be resplendent in snow-white purity ... It may be that it lacks dignity and repose, but it is typically Madeiran, a glorified and extended cottage-garden.*

Not everything in the quinta garden of C. T.-S. replicated his garden back in England, which must have greatly added to the breadth of experience and enjoyment to be had. On Madeira, he was forced to adapt, acknowledging that the two environments were very different.

> *Grass can be grown, with care and trouble, but it is not quite the same thing. And it is a question whether it is worthwhile to strive at all for that in which we cannot hope to attain a reasonable degree of success. In gardening, as in other things, which is our best course: to cultivate what suits our earth and climate to perfection – to develop our potentialities on their natural lines, or to set ourselves to fight with obstacles; to grow rhododendrons in chalky Sussex, or to foster the reluctant primrose here? Different natures will give different answers; mine would be whole-heartedly for making the best of circumstances ... So let us waste little time upon our turf here, and if we wish to see it in perfection, after its "rolling and cutting once a week for a thousand years", let us revisit the Oxford of our youth in May.*

By the early 1900s, the transition of Madeiran fazenda into flower garden was already well underway. C. T.-S. was simply following the pattern set by others before him. The process of converting banana plantation into botanical splendour was already transforming the island. A horticultural revolution was taking place, one which could trace its roots back to these early quinta gardens. Scale depended on the size of plot. In the more illustrious properties, huge landscaped gardens, set out to be viewed and admired by visitors, acquired impetus, embracing and crafting the island's unique natural garden persona.

But let us leave a more detailed look at these established quinta gardens for the days of better weather, allowing them to progress gradually to perfection, visiting some in the later chapter, 'April – The Garden in its Glory'.

*

As we know, the quintas once available for rent are no more. Some have taken on a different guise, while others have fallen into a derelict state, ever hopeful of restoration. There is nothing new about the life cycle of the quinta. History has a habit of reviving fortunes, and nowhere more so than with the quintas on Madeira.

For anyone with longer than a few hours on the island, and an interest in discovering the location of some of these old quintas in Funchal, a walk along the Rua da Levada de Santa Luzia is a good place to begin. It is one of the oldest roads in Funchal and takes its name from the earliest of the levadas to be built. A map of the town in 1910 shows this road to be on the northern perimeter, and the east-to-west transitory road of Funchal. The quintas located here were, therefore, once on the northern edge of the city.

Reaching this old road involves a tortuously steep climb on foot (buses are available) and is not for the faint or weak-hearted. The route takes one through some of the less touristy residential parts of Funchal, giving a broader perspective of the city. Once reached, the road is almost flat level. A pause is permitted, not just to recover one's breath, but for a delightful panoramic view of the bay from this elevated position.

In the nineteenth century, it would be difficult to imagine a more appropriate location for a country residence; cooler in summer and sufficiently well away from the homespun, sometimes smoky, noisy industries which would have crowded the centre of Funchal.

It's not difficult to identify the old quinta, even though some have chosen anonymity by removing the original nameplates. Impressive wrought-iron gated entrances offer a first clue, although they may be blocked in to discourage prying eyes. For some, the original quinta name is proudly displayed, like Quinta Cristovao, Quinta Martins, Quinta Keogh, Quinta Palmeira, Quinta De Santa Luzia, Quinta das Malvas. Their highly polished copper nameplates glint in the sunlight, in a manner that would not be out of place at the entrance to any big city solicitor's office.

Most are private residences, so who can blame them for seeking a little seclusion. But not all. Quinta de Santa Luzia, we discovered, is still available to be rented in its entirety. It sleeps nineteen, so one would imagine a sizeable family gathering necessary for anyone wishing to obtain the full quinta experience. Other 'retired' quinta have been put to different uses. One is now a convent retreat, and the Regional Heritage Authority has, rather appropriately, taken up residence in another.

There are many places along this road offering excellent views over the city, so it's worth stopping for a few moments to take in the view, as well as to reflect on how things would have looked a hundred years ago.

At the start of the twentieth century, along this narrow quiet road, it's easy to imagine you might have seen several cooks, returning from a visit to the city market with bags heavily laden; gardeners at work, keenly sharpening tools in preparation for another assault on the next section of the fazenda to be tamed; and nearby, perhaps, a party of quinta residents returning from an afternoon's excursion into the hills. The ladies carried by hammock hanging from a pole resting on the broad shoulders of two bearers.

A more peaceful, tranquil, spa-like setting, it would be difficult to imagine; just what the quinta residents had come here to enjoy. Along the Rua da Levada de Santa Luzia, this once discreet quinta district, you could imagine daily life would have slipped gently by, unhurried, relaxed, and utterly calm.

*

For visitors on a tighter timetable and unable to explore the island to any great extent, it's probably easiest to see some of the collective blooms and fruits common to Madeira, all set out in one convenient place.

Situated near to the waterfront on Rua Brigadeiro Oudinot (not far from the cable car station), the covered farmers' market holds a dual function. First, as a point of sale for local produce'; and second, as a showcase for cultivated flowers, fruits and fish, common to Madeira. The Mercado dos Lavradores, to give it its full title, is a place easy to wander around, without obligation, and you will not find yourself alone. It seems to have a gravitational pull for most tourists as they enter a metaphorical Garden of Eden.

Even in December and January, the entrance to the market resembles one enormous florist's shop, with individual stems and more formal displays on show. At a time when cut blooms are less plentiful, any shortfall is more than compensated for by natural foliage. Sprigs of pine seem to be a favourite, adding bulk and texture to any display, plus the most wonderfully fresh smell of the great outdoors.

Stepping further into the market, the next discovery is the fruit, spices and vegetable stalls. These days, so many of the tropical fruits will be familiar to visitors; few won't recognise the guava, passion fruit, mango and papaya, despite most of our parents having never seen them let alone sampled some. However, the custard apple (Annona), pineapple banana (Monstera deliciosa, or just 'fruto delicioso'), and the English tomato (arboreal tomato) might not be quite so familiar. Similarly, with the more seasonal figs, pitanga (Surinam cherry) and araca (Brazilian guava). They are all worth sampling, as are the small and distinctly sweet Madeiran bananas.

It is easy to see why the Madeirans' chunky little banana might be frowned upon by supermarkets in northern Europe, which seem to be wedded to uniformity in both size and appearance. The local banana has a much thicker skin than its Caribbean and South American counterparts, with a more fibrous texture. It is sweeter in taste, ideally suited to being eaten cooked or uncooked. Its structure probably makes it even more suitable for the latter purpose and it is well used when cooking fish.

The custard apple or sugar apple is especially nutritious, having a white, pulp-like flesh and a distinctive perfume. The dark seed pods are randomly spread throughout the fruit, much like a watermelon. Anyone who dislikes eating fish because of the liberal scattering of bones may equally be put off by the necessity of removing these evasive seed pods part-way through eating. Like the banana, it is a fruit which can be used raw or cooked. Pastries, puddings, ice creams, desserts, cakes and liqueurs are all made from its creamy, milky flesh.

The pineapple banana (Monstera deliciosa) looks similar in shape to an early-harvested but considerably underripe sweetcorn. The outer skin has the colour of an avocado and the scales of a closed fir cone. In taste, one can easily see why both banana and pineapple attached themselves to the name. Traces of both fight to dominate the taste buds. The fruit needs to ripen fully, almost to the point where skin and fruit agree on an amicable separation, before it is ready to eat. Once it reaches this point of maturity, however, it needs to be eaten relatively quickly.

When buying any fruit in the market, one must always be a little circumspect about what is slipped into the purchaser's bag. For anyone looking for fruits that will travel, it's necessary to check the produce before moving away from the stall, or else specifically requesting something underripe. The first pineapple banana we bought here had a shelf life calculated in minutes, but, too late, we didn't inspect the goods at the time! Many of these fruits are also available to buy in the supermarkets, where you have greater control in the selection process.

The English tomato is neither English nor a tomato. Having more the look and size of a mature plum, its inside is filled with seeds, like a passion fruit, with hardly any flesh, and has a bitter taste. Certainly not something to add to the salad bowl, it's more fruit, but with a definite need to add something to sweeten it a little.

Deeper into the market, beyond the fruit stalls, is the fish market. It's not difficult to find – just follow your nose. Located at the rear entrance, with ample ventilation to disperse the distinctive and unavoidable aroma, the displays are equally impressive. The lithe, black espada, looking for all the world to be a distant larger cousin to an eel, is unmistakable. Raised from the deepest waters, they are undoubtedly the most frequently served fish dish in a typical Madeiran tourist restaurant. I read somewhere that it is preferable for someone to taste the espada before seeing it on the fishmonger's slab. It's a fish which would not win first prize in any beauty contest! When cooked and served with banana or passion fruit, any shortcomings in the looks department are easily forgotten.

Swordfish, red mullet and tuna are also usually to be found there, often in larger proportions than you might expect to find back home. The tuna or tunny fish was a species which C. T.-S. had a long-held desire to catch.

I had nourished a hope of being able to fish with rod and line for the gigantic tunny which visit the coast in spring. The professional fishermen catch them with coarse hand-lines ... These fish sometimes weigh several hundred pounds; they are reported to fight with great dash and endurance.

Varieties of smaller local fish include bodião, which makes a good alternative to espada, and chicharro (sardine-like), served in a butter and garlic sauce, too good to miss if you are lucky enough to find them being served in a restaurant.

You will also find shellfish on Madeira; mussels, which are usually farmed; lapas or limpets can make a great starter to a meal; and caramutos – small sea snails, slow going when it comes to coaxing the morsel from its habitat.

*

And so, 'January – The Garden in Mid-Winter' passes. Temperatures in a Madeiran January can be what we might easily expect to find on any normal early English summer's day (15 to 20°C), warm enough by day but often needing an extra layer at night. So we leave the final words of this chapter to C. T.-S., who describes what we too have often found to be typical weather on Madeira during January.

Fine as has been the weather for the past four or five weeks, January is not to pass without a touch of winter. Winter for us means a strong north wind, from which Funchal is well sheltered, bringing more or less snow to the mountains, where it generally lies for a few days, and copious showers to the lowlands. The rain is not continuous but broken by short spells of sunshine, with something of the "uncertain glory of an April day" ... We amuse ourselves by grumbling at the bitter cold, and are pleased to light a fire of fir-cones in the evening ... And to the agriculturalist these plentiful showers are very grateful. They do not wash the soil away ... but sink gradually into it. And the snow on the hills will fill the springs. So the heart of the farmer is glad within him. But he always asks for more.

February. Politics and Social Change.

In his original text, the first ten pages of this chapter concentrated entirely on the events and politics of mainland Portugal. Heavily condensed here, it included the assassination of King Carlos and his son; the *"irresistibly comic Portuguese election"; "the rottenness of Government"; "a childishly absurd fiscal policy, in itself a powerful instrument of corruption";* and the need for statesmen or *"Great men"* to lead the nation forward.

The original hardback cover to *Leaves from a Madeira Garden* included an embossed image of the shield of Portugal, not that of Madeira. That it should have been so is not altogether surprising, and the clear impression given is that the politics of Portugal, at this time, were the politics of Madeira. The information available to C. T.-S. would, most likely, have come from what he observed together with the leader writers of *The Times* newspaper, conveniently in English, and as one might expect, concentrating on the wider world picture rather than the domestic politics of a small Atlantic island.

What was considered important and was reported by C. T.-S. was the effect events had on Madeira.

> *The murders of the King and his son seemed to be taken very calmly here ... I noticed that our servants, while ready to admit that the boy's death was sad, would express no regret at that of the father. The upper classes generally exhibited sorrow and horror at the deed, and the masses held in the cathedral were attended by large congregations decorously clad in mourning. But I observed that persons who appeared to be of quite respectable position took occasion to wear flaunting red ties, which, whatever their political opinions, seemed to betray a lack of decent feeling, and some apathy on the part of their fellow-citizens, in that they permitted it.*

To the authorities in Portugal, one gets the impression that Madeira was seen, politically, as a convenience, a source of income from taxation, but otherwise neglected, unless this income stream was somehow put at risk. So, for the Portuguese Government, a disaffected navy on the loose in Funchal was preferable to one in Lisbon.

> *In this strange country the comic and the tragic ever tread on each other's heels. To this tragedy the comic element was supplied by the cruiser Dom Carlos, which immediately after the murders came at full speed from Lisbon to Madeira – for the second time within two years. But on this occasion there was no question of quelling disorder here; and the wags suggested, perhaps not wholly without foundation, that the new Government, hastily formed to meet the emergency, felt happier with Funchal and not Lisbon lying at the mercy of her guns. The mere suspicion of a disaffected navy must be a perfect nightmare to shaky governments in seaside capitals.*

As for the island's political future, to C. T.-S. the success of Portugal (and therefore Madeira) depended entirely upon finding great political leaders, without which the future looked bleak.

> *Portugal needs a Lincoln to set her political house in order, a Gladstone to cleanse the stables of her finance, a Bright to raise the moral level of her public life.*

Throughout his writing, there is hardly any mention of the island's internal politics or of any machinery of government in operation. Perhaps, to C. T.-S. (who was involved in both local and – later – central government in Britain), Madeiran politics had similarities to that of a local authority, a trifle mundane in task, fulfilling sometimes tiresome administrative necessities. Policy was set down by an authoritative government in Lisbon, largely regulating the island's businesses, which were described by C. T.-S. as being *"in the hands of foreigners, chiefly English".*

Did he give any credence to the possibility that Madeira, at some time, would attain self-governance? If he did, then he kept his own counsel on the subject. The seat of power lay hundreds of miles away on the mainland. Nevertheless, he did acknowledge a strong swell of republican support.

> *How far the Republican idea has spread it is impossible to judge, but the Republican party is active and militant. The success of the French Republic during nearly forty years, and the credit which now it especially enjoys, must give a great impetus to Republican propaganda in the Peninsula.*

Again the emphasis is on Portugal, not Madeira. Clearly, he had no appreciation that within sixty-five years of his book being published,

Madeira would become an autonomous region. In fact, for a period of one month in 1931, Madeira did have an autonomous government, but a large military force from Lisbon brought this quickly to an end.

It will not come as any surprise to learn that it was also the politics of the mainland which finally brought about political change on Madeira. On 25 April 1974, a military coup took place in Portugal, known as the Revolução dos Cravos or Carnation Revolution. The flower became the emblem of the struggle, not violence, bullies or bullets. The Salazar Government was overthrown and the seeds of democracy sown.

Under the new Portuguese Constitution, Madeira's governance was placed in the hands of a newly elected President of the Regional Government and a legislature known as the Regional Assembly.

The First President of the Regional Government was elected in 1976. Alberto João Jardim was its second president, and without doubt the best known. He held office continuously from 1978 until 2015. For many years, he was one of Europe's longest-serving elected leaders.

Along with the elected Assembly of the Autonomous Region of Madeira, the effective day-to-day administration of the island is now in the hands of the Madeiran people.

The Regional Assembly Building is to be found just down from the cathedral in Funchal. Tourists can take the opportunity of an organised tour when parliament is not in session. The building itself is also very much of interest. It was once the sturdy sixteenth-century Old Customs House, with a new modern legislative assembly room added in 1987 to accommodate the elected delegates.

An election to the Regional Assembly was held in 2019. It was contested by seventeen parties, which for such a small island may seem a little excessive. Unlike the previous election in 2015, the ruling party, the Social Democratic Party (PSD), lost its overall majority, but remains in power through coalition. It took 39.42 per cent of the vote (their nearest rival, the People's Party (CDS–PP) secured 35.76 per cent). The PSD Party has been in power throughout the lifetime of the Legislative Assembly.

Turnout at the election was 55.51 per cent. Clearly, there is a diverse political allegiance amongst the population, but with a strong central core of support for the two main parties.

To the outsider, any political dissent which may exist is concealed in the Portuguese press, because outside of election time it is rarely a side of life in Madeira which is revealed to tourists. Political satire, on the other hand, aimed in the direction of the island's governing bodies or institutions (including the Church), can find a vehicle for expression when necessary. The less formal Carnival Tuesday's People Parade, for example, often chooses a 'local' issue or personality to highlight, offering comment, and sometimes ridicule or derision.

In 2018, a local priest, who had confessed to having a relationship with a woman (against the celibacy principles of the church), was singled out for attention. To the casual non-Portuguese speaking onlooker, the whole thing would have passed unnoticed. The fact that this sort of comment is capable of being made at all suggests a healthy democracy exists.

In addition to the regional legislature, local assemblies govern the major towns. As one might expect, Funchal is by far the largest. City Hall stands alongside the Collegiate Church on Praça do Municipio. The building was once a wealthy merchant's house, redesigned in the 1940s to accommodate the administrative officials, together with an assembly room for the thirty-seven elected delegates.

Much of the interior remains as first built, including the spacious watchtower. Some of the original drawing rooms are very impressive and are used today for receiving visiting dignitaries. There is also a large internal courtyard, including a fountain brought from the site of the old hospital which once stood in place of the covered market.

But what of the elected politicians from the island? C. T.-S. gives us a brief glimpse of the political classes among the Portuguese he observed at the turn of the twentieth century.

> *Compared with life, as we understand it in England, the existence of these people is very empty ... Small wonder that the game of politics, the game of pulling wires of every kind, in every direction, the game of poking political fingers into every financial and every commercial pie, should have an*

attraction for speculative and alert natures denied almost every other exercise but that which is afforded by religion. And if we add the fact that the governing classes are for the most part poor, that the hunger for office under the State as the only possible career exists to an extent which we can with difficulty understand, we may be able to picture faintly to ourselves the passion for "political" intrigue which has helped to bring the country to such a pass.

We were in Madeira during the election for the Presidency of the Regional Government which took place in March 2015. When the result became known, a small pocket of orange-scarfed supporters exhibited a greater level of jubilation than is normally found on the usually quiet streets of central Funchal. The 'game' of politics was played out in a very civil and orderly fashion, as one might expect. Only next day could be heard what sounded like a street procession passing by, possibly one of the opposition parties, reminding the new leader that he now faced a bigger challenge in winning over the hearts and minds of all the people.

The new President of the Regional Government was Miguel Albuquerque, long tipped to succeed President Jardim. A former Mayor of Funchal, in office from 1994 until 2013, he was clearly an experienced political operator. Coming from a family whose island roots run deep, his face was already well known on the streets of Funchal, an asset to any politician.

Life for these politicians is much less oppressive than might be expected for those on the mainland. On several occasions, we have seen Alberto João Jardim shopping in Funchal, acknowledging all who nodded recognition in his direction. His successor, Miguel Albuquerque, sat at the next table to us in a café just one week before his election to the Presidency. All of which tends to suggest that a semblance of normal life is still possible for senior politicians, without the necessity of round-the-clock protection.

*

Madeira is a self-governing island, but how politically charged are the Madeirans when it comes to Portuguese politics? Do they become engaged to the same extent, or has mainland politics been downgraded, with little relevance to everyday life?

In 2016, an election was held for the Presidency of Portugal. Days before voting, there were few signs that the event held too much attention. A large billboard, about five metres wide, appeared in the final week of electioneering, in front of the Municipal Gardens. It remained empty for a couple of days, then posters for three of the ten candidates were put on display. Three days before the count, there was still more blank space to be filled than there were posters, and by the morning of the election the boards had been taken away. You could be excused for thinking that lip service was being paid to an event few regarded as especially significant. Turnout at the election, however, was a little over 40 per cent, which suggests there was slightly more engagement with the voting public than enthusiasm from those charged with electioneering.

Beyond the boundaries of Madeira and Portugal lies the EU administration. The PS (Socialist Party) and Alliance won most seats at the European Parliament Election in 2019, taking 33.4 per cent of the vote, and nine seats. The PSD and Alliance came second with 21.9 per cent of the vote and six seats. Between them, they hold fifteen of the twenty-one seats available to Portugal. Turnout was 31.4 per cent, down from 33.7 per cent at the 2014 election.

*

Politics aside, C. T.-S. wrote about the Madeiran people he came to know in a social context.

> *Socially, those who have the privilege of knowing them, will find the Portuguese a very charming people. It may be that they do not feel in general much sympathy with the English, whose somewhat brusque manners and comparative want of tact must often jar on their finer susceptibilities, but it is possible for individuals of the two nations to be close friends.*

As with politics, it is noticeable he chooses to speak of the 'Portuguese' rather than 'Madeirans'. Perhaps the islanders at the turn of the twentieth century would have seen themselves as first and foremost Portuguese. Has the advent of the autonomous government, I wonder, altered this? Do people now regard themselves as Madeiran first and Portuguese a more distant second? When Portugal played a friendly international football match against Sweden on Madeira in 2017, was it the presence of the national side or of Madeira's favoured son, Cristiano Ronaldo, that attracted the crowds; or both?

*

The first settlers on the island, of course, came from Portugal.

> *To the genealogist this island must be a happy hunting-ground ... When it was first settled, in 1420, by Joao Goncalvez, surnamed Zargo, representatives of some of the chief families of Portugal accompanied him, and obtained grants of land ... Many of the great names survive to-day – Aguiar, Almeida, Camara, Correia, Freitas, Goncalvez, Leal, Ornellas, Perestrello, Vasconcellos, and others.*

To any outsider, life in Funchal seems very comfortable. An occasional person is likely to be found sleeping rough or begging in the street, but no more than in any other large city. The shops are busy and full. The private gyms seem to be thriving, although when told that it starts to get busiest around 10 a.m., you begin to realise Madeirans have their priorities set right. There is also a distinctive island culture to be found on Madeira, noticeably laid-back, relaxed and unhurried. Madeirans who have returned to the island after a time working abroad have suggested that a better quality of life, especially for the family, was the main benefit found in returning.

As one might expect on a small island, supplies of fresh produce can occasionally be slightly variable compared with a mainland location. Even the large supermarkets may run out of onions, bananas or tomatoes, but they will usually be in stock the following day. Fresh milk is possibly the one main grocery item which we must do without, but that's an insignificant price to pay.

Over time, we have noticed shops and cafés close down, but others have always been very quick to take their place. The Golden Gate Grand Café, a prominent landmark in the city from the early nineteenth century onwards, is a good example. It closed and went into administration in the autumn of 2014. Almost immediately, another café (Theo's) opened a few metres away. The Golden Gate Grand Café was such an iconic and central feature of the city, it was never likely to remain permanently closed. It reopened in 2017, along with a second Grand Café not far from it!

The notion that, as one door closes, another quickly opens, suggests that there is no shortage of capital for investment. All this is in marked contrast to the UK, where closure of a shop on the high street often seems to be an open invitation for another charity or betting shop to take its place (neither of which have I seen on Madeira; the betting culture seems to be confined to lottery draws).

Online shopping is undoubtedly dictating the future of UK high streets, but seems less evident on Madeira, although fast-food deliveries have carved out a similarly recognisable place for themselves in the home delivery market.

*

A modern feature of employment which has emerged recently in the UK is 'gig' working. It exists outside of the more usual employee/employer relationship, with people effectively classed as self-employed. An introducing 'agent' passes on jobs to perform as a single task. Taxi services and couriers were, I believe, the first to take to this form of working. I guess the term 'gig' (or event) simply implies performing one task after another.

How much of the UK economy operates on 'gig' principles is difficult to say, but when you read that the Chancellor of the Exchequer is looking at means of regulating the market, you know it has reached a level where it is impacting on income tax receipts. Unlike an employer, the notional 'agent' is not responsible for the deduction of tax from income. Nor are they required (apparently) to offer the usual employer/employee benefits. For many, 'gig' working is a full-time means of occupation and no doubt successive chancellors have come to recognise that it is too easy for these people to escape the personal taxation net.

One gets the impression that Madeira must also have its own version of a 'gig' economy too. An Uber taxi service will collect you from the airport for a lot less than the cost of a yellow cab. One might also anticipate that many of the tour guides, as well as being seasonally employed, operate on a per-job payment basis. Similarly, take, for example, the work going on in Funchal at this moment. The King's celebration has just finished and the task of dismantling the enormous infrastructure of Christmas lights and decorations, which have been in place since early December, is now in full swing. Equally, you could include any of the street clean-up operations where an army of workers is required to perform the clear-up.

Most are undoubtedly permanently employed on 'Madeira PLC's payroll' for this purpose, but one might imagine a casual workforce could easily be assembled as needed, with people engaged in these more mundane duties, slipping from one 'gig' to another, and earning a living odd-jobbing wherever they can.

If this impression is correct, then the system clearly works, but does it extend beyond the areas of low-paid manual or casual work? More recently, we have come to hear of the growth in 'Digital Nomads', professional people whose work does not require them to be located anywhere in particular, just so long as they can establish good connections to the internet. Perhaps all our work patterns are shifting, not just for Madeirans, in which case Madeira makes a perfect location to live as a Digital Nomad.

But what of unemployment? Can everyone who wants to find work succeed in that objective? C. T.-S. wrote about this too:

> *"Unemployment", in the sense that those who want work and wages cannot find them, is among a people almost entirely agricultural not a burning question; poverty is doubtless widespread, but with cold unknown and hunger easily appeased its consequences are far less severe than in less fortunate climes.*

Not surprisingly, the *"almost entirely agricultural"* work base has diminished, so, like most industrialised countries in Western Europe, levels of employment are key economic indicators. Anecdotally, we have been told that from the mid-twenties, the prospects of keeping a well-paid, low-skill job, such as at the checkouts at the supermarkets, becomes increasingly difficult. Also, the practice of short-term, unfixed hours contracts is becoming as common here as elsewhere, with one chain supposedly discarding workers after six months, presumably to avoid the rigours of some employment directive covering sick pay, holiday entitlements and pensions. Job security, again among lower-paid workers, is certainly something that is sought after, and retaining a good job is given high priority. Temporary staff, brought in to fill in for short absences, eye the prospect of a permanent position with alacrity.

According to the European jobs network EURES, from a population of a little over 250,000, "at the end of December 2018, there were

16,245 people registered as unemployed with the region's Employment Services, 31% of whom were under the age of 35".

*

Culturally, C. T.-S. found the island to be something of a 'desert'.

> *They have little literature of their own, no art, no drama, no racing, no field sports, no outdoor games – scarcely one of the multifarious pursuits which go to make up life in England for the busy and the leisured alike.*

Even today, literature seems to lack recognised inspirational figures, although C. T.-S did find one source, of unspecified origin, who had been truly inspired by the island's natural beauty.

> *Many books have been written about Madeira, but they have generally been on somewhat prosaic lines ... The poets – certainly in our language – do not seem to have found much inspiration in the island's beauties ... It has been my good fortune to light upon a remarkable book entitled "The Ocean Flower," a poem in ten cantos, published in London in 1845 ... The following verses, which describe Zargo's selection of the site for a town which he named Funchal, from the fennel which abounded there, are a fair specimen of the writer's style:–*
>
> *"For here an amphitheatre of hills*
> *Swept sheltering upwards, a fair strand around,*
> *And Zargo fixed amid three murmuring rills*
> *The island capital upon this ground.*
>
> ~
>
> *And for that on this stripe of level strand*
> *(There's round the Isle, I weep, no other mall)*
> *Grew store of fennel gay by zephyrs fanned,*
> *The Donatorio named this place Funchal."*

> *Nearly two hundred pages are filled with this sort of thing, interspersed with songs, some of which in their own way are gems.*

The most famous playwright was Manoel Caetano Pimenta Aguiar (1765–1832). Born in Madeira and awarded the Legion of Honour for services as a cavalry officer, he became a politician, but between 1815 and 1825 he devoted his life to writing historical dramas and tragedies.

The Municipal Theatre in Funchal, built in 1888, is named after the seventeenth-century blind Madeiran playwright and poet Baltazar Dias. Today, the theatre is used predominantly for live concert music rather than theatre. The building, grand architecturally, has an interior of tiered boxes on three levels surrounding the central stalls, and exudes the feel of an old West End variety theatre.

An annual literary festival takes place in March and April, so who knows, one day the island may yet inspire great modern literature. The future holds no boundaries for such possibilities. Who would have considered, twenty years ago, that from this tiny island a sports icon would emerge, golden-booted, with a personal museum, bronze statues in his home city and an international airport taking his name?

*

Arguably the two most celebrated artists from Madeira are the brothers Henrique and Francisco Franco. Born in the mid-1880s, both left Madeira to study variously in Paris, Italy and Spain, returning to the island after the outbreak of the First World War. Henrique was a painter, specialising in historical and decorative paintings and frescos. His brother, Francisco, was a sculptor. His work was widely acclaimed, with international exhibitions held in New York, Rio de Janeiro and Paris. Several of his statues of Portuguese kings survive and can be found in prominent squares in Lisbon and around Funchal. A museum devoted to their work can be found on Rua São João de Deus in Funchal.

Enthusiasts of contemporary art will find sources of inspiration at the island's newly furbished Museu de Arte Contemporânea in Calheta.

*

It seems to be from music that most of Madeira's cultural juices flow. There is a full-time Classical Concert Orchestra, with regular, well-attended concerts, held at the Baltazar Dias Theatre. In addition, with twelve chamber orchestral sections, a range of smaller concerts are sometimes held in other venues such as the Regional Assembly Building, the São Lourenço Palace and the City Hall.

Formed half a century ago, the focus of the Orchestra goes beyond entertainment. Education and the training of young musicians plays an important part, in conjunction with the Music Conservatoire.

Live traditional Madeiran folk music can be heard pretty much all year round. Playing almost exclusively for the benefit of tourists, bands of brightly clad street artists quickly grip the attention and draw a crowd with their singing and dancing. Financed by City Hall, they are there simply to entertain. I have no doubt that the iconic hats, with those distinctive pointed single straight stems, have a way of slipping into the souvenir keepsakes of many a tourist.

A more highbrow form of folk music, imported from the Portuguese mainland, however, is the music of fado or fate. Sung solo with guitar accompaniment, these rather doleful renditions reflect the sad and often bleak nature of the lyrics. For non-Portuguese speakers, some of the object of the music is, therefore, easily lost. The origins of fado are thought to date back to the fifteenth century and were usually sung by women, left alone, while their husbands were at sea. They reflect on sadness, loneliness, poverty and times of great hardship. It is not altogether surprising that such an art form should attach itself to Madeira's island culture.

A tourist's musical fado experience can best accompany a meal, at a restaurant offering live fado evenings. For an alternative, some short free concerts are held in support of the Students' Union of Madeira, at the Jesuit College in Funchal. This is a different sort of fado (Fado de Coimbra) from the academic world of the University of Coimbra in Portugal, which is sung by groups of men. Concerts are free, although they invite donations on leaving. These offer ideally sized portions, by way of introduction to this musical style.

Everyone interested in all the cultural events taking place around the island, should look for the monthly *Agenda Cultural Madeira* brochure from the Secretaria Regional do Turismo Cultural.

*

Perhaps a good topic on which to end a chapter about politics and social change is that of law and order. It was a subject on which C. T.-S also wrote.

> *There is very little serious crime in the island; aggravated offences against the person appear to be almost unknown, and robbery on a large scale, "flat burglary" is rare. You never hear of any one being molested in the town or suburbs, and you may tramp the wildest mountains and most unfrequented valleys and meet with nothing but civility from the sparse inhabitants …*
>
> *But there is a very lax state of public opinion as regards petty theft. Unless you keep watchdogs, you will have your poultry and your fruit stolen by night. The authorities seem to be reluctant to enforce the penalties against such offences. Not long since, a neighbour's gardener caught a man handing some bundles of bananas over my garden wall late at night and apprehended him as he descended himself. He called to my gardener, and together they haled the man to the police station. The case was quite clear; sections of the stalks left on the trees were produced in Court and shown to fit the bunches which the man was removing; but the judge dismissed it. I was told afterwards, I know not with what truth, that the prisoner was a very poor man, that he could not pay a fine, or for his keep in prison; and that if I had offered to pay for his board the court would have been willing to lodge him there for a week or two.*

Throughout our visits to the island, there have rarely, if at all, been any occasions when we felt law and order to be an issue. Just occasionally, reports of serious incidents do occur, usually well away from the tourist areas, and are coupled with a genuine local disbelief that such events could have taken place at all. The fact that so many of the world's international cruise lines are prepared to deposit thousands of valuable customers ashore throughout the year speaks for itself unequivocally.

Uniformed police are usually discreetly in evidence in central Funchal but appear to have little more to do other than move on the waiting taxis from an already full rank. Even on New Year's Eve, I don't think I have ever seen any arrests being made. The guidebooks often make mention of the need to beware of pickpockets, but then what country is immune from such things? A sensible traveller today knows what precautions to take, and crime is unlikely to mar one's stay.

February. Land and Sea.

For centuries, incoming tides have brought visitors to Madeira. It seems very likely that the islands were 'discovered' long before settlers first began arriving here.

> *The writers of the guide-books do not seem to have stumbled on the story, but it is recorded by Plutarch that in the century before the birth of Christ some Andalusian seamen made two islands in the Atlantic, which from the account would seem to have been Madeira and Porto Santo. They described to the Roman general Sertorius the richness of their soil, the wealth of their vegetation, their soft airs, and the equable warmth of their climate. Having heard these things, we are told, Sertorius was filled with a wonderful longing to dwell in these islands, and to live in quietness far removed from the usurpation of tyrants and the stress of war. But he was prevented by his followers, and some time after was assassinated. No later Roman made the attempt.*

Then there were sightings which might date back to the sixth-century seafarer, St Brendan. The accounts of his voyages were not recorded for another six centuries, so there is a degree of uncertainty. Some point to the Angelino Dulcert Map of 1339 as lending support to the notion that St Brendan may indeed have acquainted himself with the waters around the islands.

We do know that the first settlers arrived due to the efforts of Henry the Navigator, a fifteenth-century Portuguese prince. He was neither sailor nor navigator, but a sponsor of exploration, and a central figure in the so-called Age of Discovery.

It was one of his Captains, João Goncalves Zarco, who, along with others, discovered the island in 1419, when blown ashore in a gale on what we now know to be Porto Santo. Once discovered (or rediscovered if you prefer), settlers began to arrive between 1420 and 1425.

Thereafter, the island's strategic position meant that anyone exploring Africa, Central and South America, the Caribbean or the Far East would have passed close to the island, or called here en route.

Christopher Columbus came to Madeira because of the growing importance of the sugar trade. He married the daughter of the Governor of Porto Santo, Filipa Moniz Perestrelo, around 1479. It was his new father-in-law, we are told, who introduced the young explorer to the science of 'navigation', without which his achievements might have been less well known. He made visits to the island during his historic voyages of discovery of the Americas.

Almost three centuries later Captain James Cook, the Englishman sent to compete with the Spanish and Portuguese explorers in search of new and better trade routes to the Far East, passed through Madeiran waters during his circumnavigation of the world, sailing from Madeira to Rio de Janeiro in 1768 and again in 1772. He clearly liked what he saw, as C. T.-S. reminds us, quoting from the account of his first voyage.

> *Nature has been very bountiful in her gifts to Madeira. The soil is so rich, and there is such a variety of climate, that there is scarcely any article of the necessaries or luxuries of life which could not be cultivated here.*

A historic figure of a different kind, more prisoner than visitor, arrived by sea in 1815. He was not to set foot ashore, so one must assume his impressions of the island were snatched glimpses through a well-barred porthole, as C. T.-S recounts.

> *A more remarkable traveller arrived off the port of Funchal after dark on August 23rd, 1815. H.M.S. Northumberland, conveying Napoleon Bonaparte to his last home at St. Helena, called here for provisions ... In Madeira he had passed the last outlying speck of the world which he had striven to master, and as the vessel headed for the desolate Southern ocean, it may be that a sense of his final and utter failure at length came fully to his mind. And who may measure the bitterness of this sense to him?*

Charles Darwin called at Madeira in 1832, on his voyage to the Galapagos Islands and the Southern Hemisphere. He'd picked a difficult time, weather-wise, with HMS *Beagle* unable to make port. Not that Darwin was paying too much attention. He was feeling decidedly unwell, suffering from a bout of sickness, and had taken to his cabin, presumably with strict instructions not to be disturbed.

The ship sailed for Tenerife, but again they were unable to land. News of an outbreak of cholera in the UK had already reached the island, which would have required the entire crew to have been placed in quarantine. They did no more than turn the ship's nose south and headed on. On the return leg, Darwin chose the Azores for a short stopover, presumably having been put off by his earlier experience of Madeira and the Canaries.

*

Two other explorers of the Southern Oceans were Captain Robert Falcon Scott and Ernest Shackleton, both of whom anchored at Madeira. Scott's ship *Terra Nova* sailed from Madeira on 26 June 1910. Indeed, it was from Madeira that the Norwegian, Roald Amundsen, sent his now infamous message to Scott, *"Beg leave inform you proceeding Antarctic. Amundsen."* By then, Scott was heading for New Zealand, in preparation for his own expedition. It was the moment he first realised he had competition in his ill-fated pursuit to reach the South Pole first.

*

The African explorer Cecil Rhodes, a university acquaintance of C. T.-S., visited him here on at least one occasion, on his way to or from Africa. A stop-off at Madeira was commonplace for anyone on their way to Southern Africa during the first half of the twentieth century. Most of the touring England cricket teams would have done the same thing on their way to or from their winter playing fields.

Arguably, the greatest of these was the Yorkshire idol Sir Len Hutton. In his autobiography, *Cricket is My Life*, he gives a delightful description of his ship calling at Madeira. The now-familiar Madeiran welcome clearly left a marked impression.

> *When I arrived home I was asked what had been my queerest experience. Barring the timeless Test there wasn't time to finish, I think it was when the liner called at Madeira on the way home. Within an hour of arriving there the ship deck was practically covered with Madeira table-cloths, brought for sale by local merchants and hawkers; and the ship itself was surrounded by small boys in their little boats, diving for sixpences and threepenny bits – whatever the passengers ... threw into the water. The skill of those diving youngsters in retrieving the coins was amazing.*

In more recent times, several former British prime ministers have holidayed on the island. Winston Churchill most famously found peace and tranquillity, as well as the time to paint, in the fishing village of Camara de Lobos. He was following in the footsteps of many other prominent politicians, like Joseph Chamberlain and David Lloyd George. Dennis and Margaret Thatcher honeymooned on the island.

So, for those who tread these streets today, with less famous footprints, we simply follow in the tracks of earlier generations. Madeira is one of the most popular stop-offs for any ocean cruise liner operating in north-west Europe and the Mediterranean. For five consecutive years, it has received the World Travel Awards' accolade of 'World's Best Island Destination'.

Statistics from the Port Authority suggest that, in 2018, 293 cruise ships made Madeira a port of call, conveying over half a million passengers. Their arrival is always in orderly fashion, but in the days of sailing ships, some occasionally made a more unorthodox entrance.

Three or four years ago two boat-loads of shipwrecked mariners rowed into the port of Funchal. They landed on the pier, and commenced to relate to an excited crowd the story of their adventures, with much picturesque embellishment. They told how their vessel, a large sailing ship carrying the French flag, had sprung a leak a hundred miles to the westward of Madeira, and somewhat out of the track of steamers. They described their heroic efforts to keep her afloat, and their unceasing labour at the pumps, and how finally, with the ship sinking beneath their feet, they had taken to the boats just in time to escape being engulfed as she disappeared. So engrossed were they and their audience with this thrilling tale that until it was concluded they did not lift up their eyes to see a large sailing ship being towed into the port by a steamer. When at length observed she must have given them a nasty turn, for was she not the very vessel from which, as they had just so circumstantially narrated, they had narrowly escaped two or three days before? And indeed

"It was that fatal and perfidious bark;"

and we may feel no doubt that they greeted her with "curses dark". The inconvenient steamer had found her derelict with some awkward augur holes in her bottom, and deemed her a prize worth towing into Funchal. There are some ships that nothing will sink. What became of the poor distressed mariners I do not know; the sailing ship lay here for some time, while the

> *lawyers wrangled over the salvage, and then sailed away, doubtless in charge of a fresh crew.*

The fear of being left behind can be a constant source of worry lingering in the back of the mind of many passengers when they step ashore, no matter what the port of call. Departure times are generally inflexible, so the snake-like line of weary cruise trippers making their way back for the evening sailing schedule is a regular feature of waterfront life in Funchal.

If you miss your boat, reunion with one's possessions can be a long and complicated business with little room for amusement. Social media sites reveal many tales, from every corner of the globe, of passengers arriving on the quayside only to find the ship gone or disappearing over the horizon.

This is certainly not a modern phenomenon and goes back well beyond the days of cruise shipping.

> *Not long ago a young man and a maiden, who had made acquaintance on board, landed together from a mail-boat bound for South Africa, for a walk. Doubtless time took wings, for when they returned to the pier the steamer was gone. The girl's parents were on board, and must have been consumed with anxiety at her disappearance, as they could get no news of her until they reached Capetown. This, and not the absence of tooth-brushes, is the really tragic side of such occurrences. The young couple were hospitably entreated here, and proceeded the following week.*

We must assume that the likelihood of a week's hospitality on Madeira, followed by transportation courtesy of the next available mail packet steamer – or cruise liner – is an unlikely outcome today. Available alternatives could be few. Catch a plane to the next port of call (at your own expense) to meet up with ship and possessions or fly back home and explain to family and friends how the trip of a lifetime ended so abruptly. That is, of course, always assuming one's passport is not safely stowed inside the cabin. It's easy to appreciate why most passengers do make it back to the ship, with more than a little time to spare.

*

Earlier in his book, C. T.-S. gave his somewhat forthright views on the naming of plants. It was a theme to which he was to return. This time, his complaint was in connection with ships' names.

> *In the year 1676 [a Mr. J. C. Jeaffreson] called at Madeira ... He sailed from Gravesend in the 'Jacob and Mary', "a vessel of about a hundred and fifty tunns, 14 or 16 gunns, a square stearne, with good accommodations."*
>
> *If this vessel left something to be desired in the way of size and speed, her pleasant name atoned for much. The day of such fearsome titles as 'Cappadocian' or 'Aconcagua' was not yet. It would indeed be agreeable if one of the great steamship lines were to have the courage to revert to the old style. And surely such names as 'Darby and Joan', 'The Happy Lovers', or 'The Jolly Tripper', would amount to a gratuitous advertisement in themselves. But the modern shipowner names his ship out of the Gazetteer, and reserves his play of fancy for the decoration of the saloon, with strange and distressing results.*

Sadly, his desire for a measure of romance to be reintroduced into the naming of ships is just as lacking today. The owners, banks and shareholders, collectively holding the purse strings of these floating luxury hotels, show scant imagination when christening the capital items on their balance sheets. All too often, the ship's name corresponds to the corporate brand, with just a brief suffix distinguishing one from another. Mention of a few names like *AIDAblu*, *AIDA sol*, *Mein Schiff 1, 2, 3* or *4*, etc., *MSC Magnifica*, all regular visitors to Funchal, go to demonstrate a dearth in imagination. The days in which an element of poetry or literary craft was summoned to the occasion have sadly disappeared.

It remains for the small boating fraternity to embroider some sense of a verbal colour palette to brighten the otherwise dull harbourfront prose. Wander around the marina today, and you are likely to find the *Lovely Dawn* alongside the *Lara Jade*, with a French belle, *La Mer Michele*, near to a glistening *Starfisher*, all bobbing in communion with one another as dozens of small silvery 'snappers' dart around their slender white hulls. Who wouldn't be buoyed up stepping aboard one of these dulcet-toned, sleekly lined leisure craft?

Admittedly, they were tied up next to some rather more common, almost vulgar-sounding mooring mates. *Cash-a-Lot!* just seemed too ostentatious for my liking. One might easily picture a blazer-clad owner, wide of girth, sporting a jocular captain's cap, weighed down with gold braid, and a glass permanently to hand. Then there's *Love on the Rocks*. Was this boat the cause or the result of divorce? It's a name that simply oozes with mystery and intrigue. We are left to hope her crew concentrate less on the love and more on the rocks when sails are unfurled. As for *Alf*, we onlookers are left scratching our heads and asking, Alf who? The Great, Garnett or Ramsey?

*

For anyone who does not have to return to a cruise ship, and who has further days to spend on the island, they can idle away some time gazing on the vastness of the sea, watching as the cruise ships fade out of view. The 'Entrance to the City' pier is the perfect spot for those with "time to stand and stare". It never ceases to amaze me how hypnotic the sea and her traffic are.

Today, the usual arrivals and departures are considerably less chaotic than they would have been a hundred years ago. At the start of the twentieth century, most ships would have had to be moored out in the bay, with all the toings and froings going on around them. Tenders and boatmen ferrying passengers ashore; customs officials making for ships to clear passengers and cargo, zigzagging among the plethora of moored steamers, dodging the heavily laden bunker barges and those lazy little day boats; everyone competing for space, and not forgetting the *"diving boys"* and *"importunity of touts and traders"* anxious to take every opportunity to earn gratuities from the newly arrived visitors. At times, it must have been a frenzied sight, never the same, a constantly changing kaleidoscope, conducted to the rhythm of the tides.

For us, however, the departure of the cruise ships; the returning Porto Santo ferry; the catamarans delivering sightseers back after a day whale watching; or a couple of day fishing boats bobbing a few hundred metres out at sea are what's available to captivate the casual viewer's attention.

Compared with somewhere like the Solent or Dover, Funchal's maritime quarter is quite tame. Before long, the mind is apt to wander, eyes becoming heavy, until a drowsy and contented state overtakes.

Then, around the eastern outcrop, where wall-like cliffs stand defiantly against the sea, a tall three-masted sailing ship might slip into view. In that lethargic state, it's easy to be transported back to this same stretch of water at a very different time.

> *Before the days of steamers, wrecks must have been quite a considerable source of profit to the islanders. A southerly gale has been known to drive half a dozen ships lying in the port on shore. Steamers are able to go out to sea, where they are safe; and such a gale, especially as it sometimes does much damage to shore boats and lighters, is perhaps regarded with less favour than formerly.*

> *But the sea has sometimes brought less welcome visitors. The islands of Madeira and Porto Santo suffered much in their early days from privateers and corsairs. Next to discovering an "unsuspected isle in far-off seas," the harrying of one which somebody else had discovered and settled must have been the greatest fun imaginable. Such raids are not entirely without their modern successors, but nowadays they are not considered good form. In 1566 the town of Funchal was sacked by a large force of French freebooters, who landed on a convenient beach about three miles to the west of the town. They occupied it for fifteen days, plundering churches, convents and houses, holding citizens to ransom, and putting many, including the Governor D'Ornellas, to the sword.*

There's more than enough threat there to shake off the onset of a drowsy siesta, bringing senses quickly back to reality. So, perhaps now would be a good time to turn one's back to the sea and look upon the equally vast mountain range, and the cyclorama to Funchal's theatrical stage.

> *It is possible in Madeira to experience within the space of an hour or two quite a variety of climates, each furnished with its characteristic vegetation. From the sea-level, with its sub-tropical wealth of gorgeous climbers, its sugar-cane, mangoes and bananas, you ascend a thousand feet to find groves of oranges and lemons. A little higher you enter a region of pine-trees, with gardens where the hardy fuchsias and the hydrangeas grow to an immense size, where the ground is carpeted with agapanthus lilies, and the hedges are bright with mimosa blossom in spring. Higher still, passing from the pine-woods, you come to a moorland region faintly recalling some of the wilder parts of North Wales or Cumberland, while above are the bare and fantastic crags which have been compared to those of the Dolomites. So you may pass in a short space from the sub-tropical region to the Riviera, from*

the Riviera to Bournemouth, from Bournemouth to Carnarvonshire, and from Carnarvonshire to the Alps.

Not all those changes to the landscape are clearly visible from this seafront vantage point, but they are perhaps sufficient to motivate an inquisitive trip up into the mountain. It's not as arduous as it might seem, with a variety of means available in preference to an uphill walk, at least as far as Monte.

In January, Monte will often be several degrees colder, and seems to attract more than its fair share of cloud cover.

> *We have this year rented a cottage and garden near "the Mount", which I have already described as lying some two thousand feet above Funchal. It is rendered very easy of access by the mountain railway, and a visit to it has the advantage of affording a complete change of air. In mid-winter this region is often bathed in mist, with "the rainbow smiling on the faded storm", when the town and the lower lying country are in full sun; but as the spring advances, these uplands enjoy one of the most delightful climates in the world. The spring flowers – violets, anemones, daffodils, and the rest – which die or languish in the unvarying geniality of the litoral, flourish at this elevation in unexampled glory.*

The mountain railway has long disappeared, but the cable car and buses offer good alternatives. Monte is a popular starting point for a brief excursion on foot.

> *It lies on the very brink of a delightful ravine, the source of Funchal's easternmost river, known to the English as the Little Curral. If this valley lacks the sensational features of Madeira's wildest gorges, it is rich in all the elements of the picturesque. Up hill and down dale you walk or ride, with miniature precipices yawning below you, while rocky eminences, aping in their form the greater mountains, stand clear against the sky above.*

From Monte, as previously mentioned, the Levada dos Tornos leads further eastwards, conveniently in the direction of several tea rooms which can make for a welcome stopping place on a shortish afternoon walk. Some stretches of the levada have been closed of late, so it is always worth checking beforehand, to determine what is affected by recent rockfalls or landslides.

At Romeiros, a short distance from Monte, it is possible to ascend by road, past the Clube Desportivo Nacional football stadium (once the home of a very young Cristiano Ronaldo) and along the Caminho do Meio road. C. T.-S knew it well,

> the very steep road which ascends to the east of Funchal. This alarming road has an inclination of 23 degrees ... Crossing it, you may pass through a delightful little forest of eucalyptus trees, their smooth straight stems springing to a surprising height, and ascend to a winding levada, affording very charming views of the town, the sea, the rocky Desertas.

Not far along this road, you soon discover another winding levada which runs through the aptly named Paradise Valley. It leads to Camacha, and on to Santo da Serra from which the levada takes its name, Levada da Serra. Joining the levada path, it first skirts the southern edge of the eucalyptus forest, much of which was recently caught up in one of the devastating summer fires.

It's surprising how quickly nature adapts in such circumstances. Despite heavily blackened, charred tree trunks, buds have already been pushing out new growth. All around, fallen trees, felled to create fire breaks or just too badly damaged and not worth retaining, lie discarded, like some loggers' battlefield. A spa resort fared less well. The burnt-out shells look forlorn. Sadly, there is nothing nature can do by way of revival here, just a series of calculations for some loss adjuster to make.

Once away from this rather bleak, charred, ecological disaster area, nature resumes full prominence. In February, nothing flowers in profusion. However, just occasionally, a deep purple 'scarf' of bougainvillea lies draped haphazardly over a sunny, sheltered crag; an orange and red carpet of nasturtiums, creeps on its belly over any piece of wasteland having unobstructed views of the sky; and agapanthus leaves, for the time being withholding fresh blooms. In later months, it will be admired, then taken for granted, just a part of nature's 'fixtures and fittings', so great is their number. Then an occasional, unblemished, long-stemmed, lone arum lily, fresh from its brief winter siesta, stands serene like nature's statuesque version of a bride on her wedding day. These are just some of the sights which await visitors to Paradise Valley, even in February.

The paths of the Levada da Serra are well worn, mostly by feet, although very occasionally shared by two-wheeled pedal-pushers. But then there have always been a variety of modes of transport in use when people take to the hills.

> *You may proceed to the hills ... on foot or on horseback; or in the ancient Madeira mode you may be carried by men in a hammock slung on a pole. The hammock and the palanquin were formerly the chief means of locomotion for ladies in town or country; the hammock is still used for mountain excursions, and by aged priests when visiting their parishioners. A combination of riding and walking is the pleasantest method for those who are equal to it.*

Eventually, the levada arrives at the outskirts of Camacha.

> *A very pleasant village indeed it is, lying over two thousand feet above the sea-level, on a spur of the higher hills, a few miles to the east of Funchal. It was formerly much resorted to in summer by those English whose business retained them in Madeira, as is attested by the presence of some agreeable villas, now little used. The railway which ascends to "The Mount" directly above Funchal now makes that locality more convenient as a residence in hot weather. Camacha possesses among other attractions a level tract of good turf on which many a cricket match has been played. It might be mistaken for the green of an English village but that it lies on the very brink of a deep and picturesque ravine.*

Despite several visits, we have yet to hear the sound of willow on leather-clad ball. Most people visiting Madeira in the winter season will probably not venture to Camacha, despite it being relatively close to Funchal. Some excursions to the east and north-east of the island may include a brief stopover on the day trip's return leg. Its elevated position (higher than Monte) means the temperature is likely to be a few degrees cooler than at the coast, but some benefit is to be found. The cool conditions make it well suited to growing daffodils, bunches of which may be for sale in the small market square. Most of what Camacha has on offer for tourists seems to be from a bygone age.

> *In this hamlet and its neighbourhood is made much of the wicker-work – chairs, tables, sofas, and other articles – which fills the shops of Funchal. Enormous quantities are purchased by the passengers of passing steamers; and it is not unknown at charity bazaars in England. It is carried down the steep mountain road to the town chiefly by women, who will bear,*

balanced on their heads, a surprisingly heavy and unwieldy mass of tables and chairs.

It's unlikely that *"enormous quantities"* of wickerwork furniture and baskets are high on anyone's gift list in the twenty-first century. One wonders what the cruise operators would make of it, if the tradition were to be revived. Cruise passengers, of course, have the luxury of less rigid luggage restrictions. You might imagine one could quickly be imposed if thousands of their passengers suddenly developed an interest in carrying wickerwork back home with them.

Regional tourism on the island often seems to lack Funchal's energy and imagination. Perhaps there are signs that this is recognised. The Contemporary Art Museum has recently relocated from Funchal to a new gallery in Calheta.

Beyond Camacha, the levada leads on to the mountain village of Santo da Serra, a very good day's walk from Monte. The village has a Saturday market which has the feel of a traditional farmers' market, as you might expect to find in many market towns throughout England.

Under makeshift shelters, you get the clear impression that the eyes of the stallkeepers belong to those who have watched over the crop, from planting to harvesting. Weathered, lined faces, exposed to the toil of planting, weeding and watering, now share in the less arduous and equally rewarding reaping of the harvest. It is where the results of their labours come to fruition.

Because of the island's prolonged growing season, there tends to be much more justification for an all-year-round harvest celebration on Madeira. Santo da Serra's weekly gathering is much more than a mere market. It's as much a social event, with villagers and outsiders combining to enjoy the tasks of choosing, negotiating, buying and selling. As might be expected, leisure time is also given to enjoying a glass of poncha which complements the occasion well; as does crumbling the shell of a freshly roasted chestnut; or de-husking marinated lupin seeds. A special touch is required here, squeezing the lupin seed between thumb and forefinger to prize out the incarcerated yellow legume, and it takes practice. Once rid of its outer skin, the slightly salty taste gives a strong reminder of the island's links with the sea and is enjoyed in much the same way as those from Mediterranean countries enjoy olives.

Not everything at Santo da Serra market is horticultural. The adjacent stalls across the road sell clothes, toys, glasses, bags, belts and the like, and this section has a markedly less authentic 'feel' than its agricultural near neighbour. One feels the produce market could easily exist without the other, but not vice versa.

Anyone choosing to walk along the Levada da Serra and Paradise Valley in the opposite direction ends up at Monte, and will have the chance of returning to the waterfront by cable car, or via one of the renowned wooden sledges. As we know, a return to Funchal courtesy of the familiar "running car" was an adventure just as familiar at the time of C. T.-S.

The earliest use of this form of transport seems to date back to around 1850 in Monte and quickly caught on as a popular tourist attraction. Chief Scout Robert Baden-Powell (a bronze bust of whom stands in Rua João Tavira, Funchal) is reported to have enjoyed the ride during a visit to the island, as this extract from the 1962 edition of *Boys' Life* published by the Scouts Association of America records.

> *On the Portuguese island of Madeira, Baden-Powell joined a number of other tourists in the island's famous attraction: the wild ride in wooden sleds down the cobblestone mountain street, steered by a couple of hefty guides.*

So, let's leave this chapter in the capable hands of the running car operators, the *correiros* or the two-man, wicker 'taxi' drivers who

> *return in "running-cars" down the Mount Road. These cars are, I believe, peculiar to Madeira. They are made of wickerwork and mounted on sledges, and descend the steep roads around Funchal very rapidly, chiefly by the force of their own momentum. They are guided by two men by means of ropes fixed to the front of the car, and where propulsion is necessary, the men stand with one foot on the back of the car and push with the other behind.*

It is an experience which surely must be sampled by everyone, at least once!

February. Taxes – Monopolies – Poverty.

I would imagine any chapter, no matter what the book, having the title 'Taxes – Monopolies – Poverty', may at first sight (and on many subsequent sightings too) appear to offer little in the way of fertile ground, even for "irrelevant jottings". I have a fear that somebody beginning a two-week stay might easily read the title, raise an eyebrow and quickly thumb through to the start of the next section! It's the sort of subject from which we'd all hoped to escape, if only for a short while? The topic, therefore, calls for a very light touch, which I hope the reader will find here in good measure. It's the chapter, perhaps above any other, that lays bare the stark differences between Madeira today and one-hundred-and-ten years ago.

In the hope that we have some readers brave enough to venture on, the subject's inclusion in the original text also gives further insight into the interests of C. T.-S. As previously touched upon, someone capable of taking a continuous four-month break during the year, who is not yet retired, would certainly have needed a settled income, perhaps with an established business investment portfolio, requiring only periodic attention. One might also imagine that it would still have needed a regular 'diet' of fresh investment opportunities, so the supply of international news, analysis and fresh prospectuses to mull over, serving to maintain the portfolio's continued good health, would also have been a necessity.

In the early twentieth century, it is difficult to imagine from what he had written that C. T.-S. would have invested heavily in any local Madeiran enterprises. Nor that the make-up of the Madeiran economy would have added much to his knowledge of business acumen.

> *The commercial conditions existing in this island afford a melancholy example of the evils of State interference in business matters. Of unrivalled climate, with a soil of great fertility, and lying within a few days' steam of the greatest markets in the world, it is yet prevented by a vicious fiscal system from enjoying the wealth which is its natural due. There is no question here of the encouragement of young and struggling industries by a moderate scheme of Protection, and it is not necessary in this connection to*

consider under what circumstances, if ever, Protection is beneficial. Two facts strike the observer: firstly, the apparent desire of the Government to tax everything that can be taxed, regardless of consequences; and secondly, the extraordinary state of things which may be brought about by monopolies created in the supposed interest of one set of cultivators, but probably originating in the desire of the politicians to have their fingers in every possible pie ... The Authorities do not appear to understand that an export trade is one of the chief sources of wealth; that people cannot live "on taking in each other's washing"; or that exporters have to compete in foreign markets with the producers of other countries; that the price they obtain for their wares is chiefly regulated by that competition; and that it is to the interest of the whole community that they should not be driven out of those markets by the artificial raising of the cost of production. "Here is an industry, come let us tax it to death" seems to be their motto.

His financial interests would have lain elsewhere. One can assume, therefore, that sightings of the next package steamer would have been greeted with great interest. These seaborne arrivals were his main source of information, with fresh supplies of newspapers, letters and other mail, keeping him in touch with important business requiring his attention.

We know from earlier accounts of life on the island that there were several libraries in Funchal, to which membership could be obtained, giving access to copies of the latest major English, French and Portuguese newspapers. C. T.-S. makes no mention of using these; instead, we can assume that someone would have been tasked with attending the arrival of the next steamer, to collect the latest bundle of news, returning hot-foot to the quinta.

In this secluded isle we get our newspapers in a lump once a week. This serves to heighten the effect of their terrific contents. At home the perusal of different editions hour by hour produces a comparatively listless frame of mind; interest is staled by custom. Here six days of calm, broken only by inadequate press telegrams from Lisbon, which are generally more concerned with the numbers drawn in the State lottery, and such matters of urgent local interest, than with the politics of Europe, are succeeded by a day of shock. Some persons of well-regulated mind are able to read their papers in due succession, one a day, and so to take their daily dose of news like civilized folk. The more usual practice is to swallow the whole lot – to sup full of horrors – within an hour or two of the arrival of the mail.

So, for the next few hours, we can assume C. T.-S. would probably have withdrawn from the tasks occupying his time that day, to spend a while blinkered, focused, totally 'in the zone', concentrating on the latest dispatches.

It is interesting to wonder how enviously C. T.-S. might have looked on the 'global village' of today with its modern communication links.

> *It is almost incredible that under these circumstances ... there is no telephone system. If you want to send a message you send your servant to run with it, and if he happens to look in at his club, and to take part in a prolonged rubber, you will not see him again for some time.*

The availability of good Wi-Fi and broadband (we have noticed no appreciable difference in communications in Funchal from the mainland) has certainly made it easier for someone to work from the island, as has already been discovered with the advent of the 'Digital Nomads'. Given the same facilities, I wonder how long it would have been before C. T.-S. might have concluded that being constantly available to all and sundry also had some noticeable drawbacks. From what we have just read, we can assume he quite enjoyed the "*six days of calm*" before the next bundle of news arrived. In business, too, he might have concluded that things had become just a little too invasive, and that a return to the regular, conveniently spaced arrivals of the packet steamers was a far more relaxed and convenient way of getting the latest news.

It is difficult to imagine him wishing to change places with us. His preference might have been to accept a marked reduction in news, relieved of the necessity of regularly checking such things as incoming emails, not to mention the trivia that can surround social media. There is a certain reassurance to be had in the knowledge that no news is good news, with all the advantages to the human constitution such forced 'deprivation' brings.

*

As previously mentioned, given his background, it's not altogether surprising to learn that taxes and monopolies might have been a topic of interest to him. He begins the chapter with a forthright description of the state of Madeira's economy.

> ... with the exception of certain minor articles, such for example as furniture and boots, few things in general use are manufactured in the island. It must be acknowledged that they act as protective of certain industries on the mainland of Portugal; but to judge from the predominance of foreign (chiefly German) goods in the shops, this protection is of no great effect. The duties are in practice rather restrictive than protective. Every one gets in the way of doing without many things which in other countries are in quite ordinary use. And to some extent they account for the backward state of the island in such matters as sanitation. The enormous duty on iron pipes, for example, discourages very effectually private enterprise in the laying on to houses of water from springs, and so on ...
>
> In spite of everything the State can do to cripple foreign trade, and the fact that the most important export, wine, is a declining factor, a good deal of foreign money comes into the island. The coaling, watering and provisioning of calling ships employ much labour; there is an ever-increasing influx of visitors during the winter and spring; and the salubrity of the climate tempts many Portuguese who have made money in tropical countries to make it their home on retiring from business.

In the last quarter of the twentieth century, however, something approaching a modern tax haven has developed on Madeira, thanks to the EU-approved Free Trade Zone, clearly not something C. T.-S. could have predicted from what we have just read.

The Autonomous Region of Madeira is outrunning anywhere else in Portugal, putting it among the most prosperous areas in Europe. Although subject to the same EU regulations, directives and decisions, Madeira benefits from allowable regional adjustments.

The Madeira International Business Centre (IBC) provides incentives of greatly reduced levels of corporate tax for international investors with the potential for new job creation initiatives.

Two areas to have benefited most from the IBC are the financial services sector and ship registration. International trading platforms; financial services in shares and investments; the management of international patents and branding; as well as management and marketing consultancy; software development; all have found a niche within the island's business community.

The Madeira Shipping Register is open to international shipping, yachts and offshore platforms, and provides all the usual shipowner advantages of offshore flagging. It's now the fourth-biggest ship registry in Europe.

The Madeiran economy today leans heavily towards the service sector (tertiary sector), which accounts for around 84 per cent of global output. Industry (secondary sector) follows at around 13 per cent, and agriculture (primary sector), seen by C. T.-S. as having potential, *"with a soil of great fertility, and lying within a few days' steam of the great markets in the world"*, falling into low single-percentage figures.

With a population of a little over 250,000, the number of adults over 65 and those under 15 years of age make up about 30 per cent of the population, leaving a good number to stoke the economic fires. Clearly, Madeira has yet to feel the full effects of the demographic ageing time bomb facing many other Western economies. With a good supply of labour and a sound infrastructure in place, most things necessary for a robust economy are here. All of which goes to emphasise how far Madeira has progressed from the island C. T.-S. found on his visits.

> *There is no money to provide even the most ordinary requirements of a civilized country. Roads, bridges, water-supply, drainage, hospitals, asylums, schools – in all these departments Madeira is a century behind the age. If you ask why, there is no answer but "We are too poor." Good heavens! how do the Portuguese imagine that peoples inhabiting countries which lack almost all the advantages of theirs furnish themselves with these necessaries of life and a hundred others?*

Today, Madeira has an infrastructure, with all the modern support services, to stand alongside most places in western Europe. In a little over a century, it has made up the ground and no longer remains *"behind the age"*. Much of this has taken place in the second half of the twentieth century, when the international airport and more regular cruise visitors enabled tourism to blossom, bringing increased imported wealth and a much-needed source of year-round employment. But this alone would have been insufficient to account for the island's change in fortunes. Wealth from the sugar and wine trades had been here for centuries.

Perhaps the real difference today lies in the fact that, in the past, this wealth was concentrated in a few hands. The new wealth is channelled much more into providing such things as better education, training and health care for the general population, to meet the needs of this new emerging economy. It's a change which has been quite remarkable and achieved over a relatively short period.

*

The island is divided into eleven administrative areas: Calheta, Câmara de Lobos, Funchal, Machico, Ponta do Sol, Porto Moniz, Ribeira Brava, Santa Cruz, Santana, São Vicente and Porto Santo. In all respects, statistics for Funchal dwarf everything. Approximately half the population live and work in and around Funchal.

It is tourism, and especially the cruise and leisure industry, which is now the mainstay of the modern Madeiran economy. Most of this has only developed appreciably in the second half of the twentieth century, but this would not have come as too much of a surprise to C. T.-S., who saw the potential.

> *A stranger may ask in surprise why Portugal, and especially Madeira, are poor. It is obvious that this island is one of the most favoured spots of the earth's surface. Its genial climate, its fertile soil, its ample rainfall, its situation on the lines of route from South and West Africa and South America to Europe, and from North America to the Mediterranean; its possession of plentiful labour – all these factors combine to promise an exceptional prosperity of State and individual alike. This promise is not fulfilled ... Even the provision of "up-to-date" hotel accommodation for visitors appears to be rendered impossible. The companies which have been during recent years crowding the health resorts of Europe with first-class hotels and restaurants have left Madeira alone, and the wealthier class of travellers, which is prepared to pay for its comforts and might bring much profit to the island, is discouraged from visiting it.*

If we were able to show C. T.-S. the hotel district west of Funchal today, he would undoubtedly feel vindicated. Having received the necessary investment, Madeira competes with island resorts anywhere.

It does so by recognising that individual visitors represent a highly valuable income stream. Everyone, from the tour guides conveying those preferring to be escorted; to the open-top bus services offering a day ticket to 'free roamers'; and the coffee bar owners, museum keepers, gift and fashion shops, restaurants, hotels, taxis; they all depend, directly or indirectly, on these swarms of pleasure seekers. The city bids each one a cheery welcome and a fond farewell, safe in the knowledge they are likely to return or that another cruise vessel or aircraft will shortly appear, maintaining a cycle of continuity.

But these regular arrivals are not inevitable. They require a level of service and Madeira knows it. Nothing is taken for granted, with acutely fine-tuned levels of attention paid to each detail.

Unlike the ships of C. T.-S.'s day which, as we have heard, he described as having the *"temporary character of pleasure ships"*, today's cruise vessels are purpose-built, and far from feeling *"ashamed of their jobs"*, brashly flaunt their grandeur. Floating hotels, with every conceivable modern facility, open-air cinemas, theatres, whirlpools, splash pools, restaurants, gyms, medical centres, they locate and relocate like free-spirited disciples of Poseidon, content to blend into whatever backdrop happens to present itself next.

Occasionally, the noise of the open-air cinema or disco spills over the ship's side like an audible slick. One is inclined to think they never give too much thought to the island's inhabitants, nor suffer any feeling of guilt when this occurs. Such is the price the island pays for welcoming these lucrative floating wanderers into their waters and inviting them to secure mooring lines onto their jetties.

The cruise operators are aware of the value they represent to the island's economy and impose themselves in a way, one feels, that in the days of C. T.-S. might just have been checked. That said, he was under no illusion about the importance of this passing trade to the island.

> *The amount of money left by passing steamers must be very considerable. In the palmy days of Johannesburg, the homeward-bound Cape mail, with much money burning holes in many pockets, must have been a veritable gold mine. And nowadays huge steamers taking American tourists to the Mediterranean call here and remain thirty–six hours.*

Cruise ships rarely seem to spend more than daylight hours on a visit to the island before putting to sea again. Whether through choice, or on economic grounds, minimising unnecessary overnight port dues, their stay is usually brief. Transatlantic cruises (other than those on a round-the-world schedule), bringing American tourists to the island, have largely disappeared. Undoubtedly, it's more cost-effective, and possibly more comfortable, for Americans to fly into Europe to join a cruise rather than experience an Atlantic sea crossing. Portuguese, English and Germans make up the bulk of the nationalities visiting the island.

Despite the Madeirans' dependence on these ephemeral guests and their importance to the economy, it must be a source of concern that today's large cruise ships are quite so self-sufficient. They arrive with thousands of passengers, tie up alongside, and wait to be entertained. One is never especially aware of these ships restocking or even refuelling as they would have in the past. The requirement is simple: 'entertain' us, or we might go elsewhere in future!

With no big demand for coal to fuel the return leg, these sea 'whales' carry enough bunkers for the remainder of the cruise itinerary, or sufficient to enable them to be selective as to where they make a refuelling stop and obtain the most advantageous price. No big demand for fresh food either, as their chillers and freezers probably have the capacity to cope with the demands of an entire cruise, if it is a relatively short one, such is the extent of their bulging self-sufficiency.

*

For anyone conducting business on Madeira, you could imagine there to be something of a village-like feel to commercial life. With most businesses concentrated in Funchal, it must be difficult for any organisation to do anything which goes unnoticed. A company restructuring, professional reputations, new ventures; it's easy to imagine news spreading quickly, and trying to keep anything 'under wraps' must be a thankless task. In larger mainland conurbations, this would be much less of a problem.

As already mentioned, there doesn't seem to be any shortage of readily available investment cash, in either the business or the residential property sectors. In addition to EU grants, there seems to be a ready supply of money from overseas. Businesses and individuals from Russia, Brazil and Venezuela find Madeira an ideal place in which to relocate money, content to buy at high prices, with assets allowed to remain dormant if necessary. High property prices, especially in central Funchal, seem to have been maintained by the influx of foreign capital. Some of this investment may bring new employment opportunities, but it can also have the usual effect of depriving the young of their own personal investment opportunities, especially where accommodation is concerned.

For too many, as in London, the centre is already too expensive to contemplate a purchase. Young couples wanting to buy their own homes invariably look outside of Funchal when making their first purchase. This can seriously impact on the city's character, especially where once-residential areas are acquired for more office space.

To tourists, the attraction of any city is the feeling that it is 'lived in'. Commercial quarters can too easily become ghost towns at evenings and weekends. It's why the older parts of Funchal, with the painted doorways, have far more appeal than the glass-fronted, modern, under-let, part-occupied apartment blocks and offices.

*

The shops in Funchal have something of a 1970/80s UK High Street feel to them. Most outlets appear to be individually owned, rather than part of a franchise or chain. To look at any high street in the UK today, you would be hard-pressed to say exactly where you were, as they all look so much alike. The individual shops in Funchal give out a much stronger, distinctive statement and help create the city's unique character.

There are exceptions, of course, with chains like Opan bakeries being an obvious example. Similarly, the major Portuguese supermarkets have a firm foothold in the capital. Names such as Pingo Doce and Continente must cater for the bulk of a family's weekly food shopping, although we have seen a few very small independent fresh grocery outlets open in the last couple of years. Some of the international chains are inevitably here too. Pizza Hut, Subway and H&M have all set up stall, but they are considerably outnumbered by local enterprise.

There are several out-of-town shopping malls, Madeira Shopping and Forum Madeira being the largest, either of which can occupy any tourist's attention on a cloudy day. Those looking in search of a new wardrobe will invariably be rewarded.

The shops in the centre of Funchal tend to be deceptively small-fronted, but this has always been the case. In the book *Madeira, its Climate and Scenery*, first published in 1850, the following description was given of shops in Funchal.

> *Most of the shops in Funchal are to be found in the streets adjoining the Custom-house; their outward appearance is by no means prepossessing, being generally in confined situations, and without any show, or even a window to set off their goods.*

Once inside, however, this diminutive appearance can give way to a spacious interior, much larger than the entrance suggests is possible.

On-street shop signage and advertising also give a low-impact look to the shops and seems to be much more discreet than in the UK or the mainland. This may be due to an inherent cultural preference for unobtrusive marketing or evidence of a tight hand on the tiller of regulation over what is permitted. A sign projecting into the highway (as opposed to a facia over a shop door) is distinctly minimal. Banks and chemists use this projecting advertising, but otherwise it is seen very little, which seems much more in keeping with the city's low-impact advertising persona.

There is some indication this may be under threat. Along the Avenida do Mar, bus shelters have recently acquired backlit billboards, and there are a couple of purpose-built illuminated street advertising structures. All of which suggests that, given the chance, the marketing men have a desire to creep ever further into the main thoroughfares of Funchal.

A rather incongruous giant outdoor TV screen appeared a few years ago, beside the founder's statue and within sight of the city's cathedral doors. A very odd place to choose, one might think, and how it came to be sited there might make for interesting research. Surrounded by trees, it almost looks as if, given half a chance, it would pull on some of those branches to hide its embarrassment. At present, it does seem to restrict itself to highlighting places of interest. That said, it's a short step away from selling advertising space, which would be a great pity.

It does nothing for me as a tourist, other than create a modern carbuncle in an otherwise cherished and historic corner of the city. I'd sign any petition to have it removed.

Overall, low-impact advertising seems to be the norm. The recent opening of a shop near to where we stay is a good case in point. It was a new addition to a small chain, and one large enough for a government official to attend the opening. At the time it opened, there was no fascia signage over the shop at all. Customers looked through the windows to see what they were selling. Ten days later, a sign did eventually go up above the entrance.

Did it matter that the sign was late in arriving? Coming from a culture where someone's job might have been on the line for not having it there on time, we tend to look at such things with a different perspective. On Madeira, the island's culture views such things with a much more relaxed manner. Why fuss over a few days? It's a lovely philosophy for the island to hold on to and, more than anything, instils the right balance to the quality to life here.

*

Madeira has had long-established associations with other island communities. Jersey and Guernsey have some of the largest Madeiran expatriate communities in Europe, and St Helier in Jersey is twinned with Funchal. Commercial links go back centuries. It is reported that wine was being shipped from Guernsey to Madeira during the eighteenth century, possibly taking advantage of the unique fortifying process.

In the early second half of the twentieth century, many Madeirans travelled to the Channel Islands in search of work during the summer months, when tourism on Madeira was at a low point, enabling them to return to Madeira for work during the winter season. Not surprisingly, many came to make the Channel Islands their home.

Gibraltarians were offered sanctuary on Madeira during the Second World War. In an age when globalisation tends to look down on the small, whether it's enterprises or communities, who can blame Madeira for creating their own informal association of sorts with similar sea-locked small island communities?

March. The Garden in Spring.

A notable feature of the past month has been the flowering of a native plant, the "Pride of Madeira", Echium fastuosum. It grows wild on the sea-cliffs, and in greater luxuriance in gardens. From a mass of grey foliage it throws up a number of torch-shaped heads of a beautiful blue-grey colour, according well with the rocks or walls over which it loves to hang ...

Freesias are now in full blossom, and the air is sweet with their delicious perfume ... The yellow blossom of the mimosa trees has about it a very strong suggestion of spring.

Among climbers the Bougainvillea is now in its fullest perfection ... And shortly we shall enjoy what is perhaps the noblest of our flowers, the upstanding cream-white bells of Solandra grandiflora ... Here it will fling itself along a wall, or over a roof, in unrivalled luxuriance. If it has a fault it is that its splendid blooms too quickly fade ...

Yet perhaps with our wealth of roses, varying indeed in profusion but never lacking; our gorgeous tropical climbers; our masses of scarlet geranium, and brilliant pelargonium; our hedge of sweet peas; our beds of delicate begonia; of euphorbia, azalea, fuchsia, lantana, salvia, linum and many another never-failing flower.

Spring in Britain is wholly different in character to what we find on Madeira. At home, as daylight hours lengthen, with the sun making more promising and frequent reappearances, we earnestly look for the first signs of recovery. Outdoor temperatures reflect minor, subtle changes. From time to time, winter may defiantly tighten its grip once more, refusing to let go. But to plant life, their ability to judge minimal changes more finely tuned than our own, even the smallest variation becomes significant. The first visible signs come as the spring flowers, crocuses, snowdrops, daffodils, tulips, all gently push their 'blind' closed heads skywards. Only when they eventually reveal themselves can we be truly sure that spring has arrived.

People living in one of the south-coastal resort towns are first to recognise the advent of spring bidding a fond farewell to winter's chills. From here, it gently rolls out its fresh seasonal tide, pushing northwards, at no more than a gentle walking pace, unhurried, oblivious to our wish for a speedier transition.

But what of the Madeiran spring?

> *In a sense we have no spring; we have no winter to make a true spring possible. For that splendid awakening from a long sleep we must go north – to England it may be in late April or early May; better still perhaps to Norway in early June. We have a semblance of it in the upland gardens ... But in the lowlands spring smiles perennial – wherefore it is not spring.*

The flowers we associate with spring and the start of a new growing season are unlikely to be found in central Funchal.

> *We miss that peculiar freshness of the spring-flowering shrubs, the sudden burst of colour in the rock garden, the rainbow tints of the spring bulbs. Even tulips are implacable. Such spring flowers as we have, if they have not bloomed at intervals during the winter months, lack the foil which the still wintry aspect of the surrounding vegetation supplies at home ...*

> *[In Madeira] you can grow out of doors everything cultivated in a cool greenhouse in England ... Where we break down is with plants whose health requires a cold snap. To find the spring flowers – the anemones, the daffodils, the violets – in perfection, we must go to an altitude of 1500 to 2000 feet above the sea, where winter nights are cold, and snow sometimes falls, though not to lie.*

A Madeiran spring, if one may call it so, is less distinct. The transitions from winter to early summer almost coincide. Spring is no more than the first appearance of bloom and blossom, some of which will emerge and remain for the summer's duration.

The season is also heralded by an increase in activity in the parks and gardens of Funchal. It's a delight for any visitor, not just to gaze at the flowers and plants shaking off winter's demeanour, but as much to watch the teams of gardeners at work, entrusted with their upkeep.

Having spent most of my life living in a town designed by the founder of the Garden City Movement, Sir Ebenezer Howard, I see some slight similarities with Madeira. The attention given to tending public green spaces mirrors exactly what the original New Towns of the early twentieth century looked to advance in the UK; the creation of a town with a garden at its heart.

In the 1950s and 1960s, labour in the UK was both plentiful and affordable, with the Parks and Gardens Department one of the biggest workforces on the payroll of the town council. Today, a gesture is made towards the original Garden City concepts, with concentration given to preserving the appearance of just a few prominent and selected areas. Sadly, the cost of maintaining the original number of public spaces to the same high standards has simply become unaffordable. Other priorities have acquired a louder voice, thereby weakening one of the fundamental characteristics of Garden City ideals.

Funchal, too, recognises the importance of maintaining public parks and gardens to a high standard, seeing it as central to the tourist appeal. What's more, it puts in place the resources to properly fund their upkeep and maintenance. The Municipal Gardens (once the site of a Franciscan monastery) is a good example.

Today, it's literally swarming with gardeners in their two-tone green overalls, pruning, weeding, transplanting, building new retaining walls and, yes, even in March, watering. Beds are tended by rote. Weeds grow in profusion, possibly more so than in colder climates, and are evicted before they become established. In the same way, last year's abundant foliage requires thinning, with a seasonal cut and trim. It's the horticultural equivalent of a change of bedlinen, giving variety and a fresh appearance.

It's gardens such as these which form a part of the tourists' 'entertainment'. Many visitors are apt to return, and, like the Christmas decorations, they would hardly expect to come to see identical displays year after year. It's the variation that repeat visitors seek out, taking stock of what's different this year. When they do so, they revive memories of previous visits, at the same time as grafting on new memory shoots from this year. They take great comfort from the simple and assured continuity of it all. Change is usually only slight, subtle, and easily assimilated.

Where there is a small lack of variation, however, it is in the design and layout of these tended beds and borders. For someone like C. T.-S., they often lacked originality.

> *From the gardener's point of view it is all too neat; it lacks that element of roughness which suits a garden best; but neatness and symmetry are Portuguese ideals ...*
>
> *This passion for regularity is one of our minor garden troubles. If you tell your gardener to plant out fifty stocks in a bed, you will find them in rows at equal distance, carefully measured to an inch ... He will perhaps learn in time that you like them planted irregularly in clumps, but the practice will never have his approval, and he will regard it as only one more of your incomprehensible fads.*

Symmetry still rules here, so far as the layout of these plots is concerned. Borders are invariably knife-edge straight, edging stones in regimental alignment, plants in parade-ground order, rarely randomly sited. In many ways, they mirror in conformity the same straight lines around the traditional doors and window frames of the older-style houses, so perhaps we are witnessing a very deep cultural trait.

The municipal gardeners never appear to consult formal plans of what plants go where. Nevertheless, you have the clear impression that the designers have already been at work. Instructions are being followed. Some sort of arrangement plan has been imprinted on the minds of the men who are engaged to bring it into effect. Or perhaps they follow the pattern set by earlier generations, whom they watched and from whom they learnt their trade.

The attention given to these municipal spaces is possibly even more necessary now, with the decline in the amount of wild, flower-bedecked open spaces, once a feature of the Funchal hillsides.

Fresh horticultural activity is not only conducted at a municipal level. You sense, at this time, that local gardeners are beginning to pay more attention to their own flowering plots. Yesterday, as we travelled by bus, a lady boarded, holding several armfuls of white Easter lily bells, the arum lily. It took all her time to just maintain control of this precious bundle. Together they swayed, like tall grass in the wind, she valiantly struggling to keep hold of her charges while maintaining a firm hand-hold as the bus wound its way up the snaking hillside. Taking an offered seat was entirely out of the question. Maybe there was enough space for her or the flowers, but not both. I can't believe these blooms were for her personal use – there were far too many – and I assume they would have been gathered, hand-picked, ready for sale in the marketplace the following day, or perhaps to decorate the interior of her local church.

*

In his horticultural pursuits, C. T.-S. enjoyed experimentation, trying to see to what extent he could adopt an English-style garden on Madeira.

> *I have made a valiant attempt to form a little rock garden on English lines, and it must be owned with reluctance that it is a complete and utter failure. I did not venture to hope that many "Alpines" would put up with the conditions of this climate, but I was not prepared for the behaviour of some of the rock-plants which are almost weeds in our rockeries at home. Of the numerous kinds ... which I imported, not many have survived the summer, and not one has really flourished. To my surprise, gentians have lived and look fairly healthy; but they show no signs of flowering. Some plants change their habits under the new conditions; the common cat-mint, which on the Sussex chalk grows into a respectable shrub, here creeps along the ground with great humility ... It is, I think, not so much a matter of climate as of soil. In dry weather the earth here cakes almost to the consistency of stone and these rock-plants may be unable to extract from it the moisture they require ... So if one is to have a rock garden, one must probably fall back for its denizens on such succulent plants as cacti, which contain their own supply of water within themselves ... but with all their beauty they will not equal in interest the spring glory of the English rock garden.*

Many of the plants found in the gardens of Madeira will be familiar, but not always appearing as they do in an English setting. A good example is the poinsettia, an imported indoor pot plant that we force to endure the short Christmas season, all the while knowing its inescapable fate. Here on Madeira it's frequently to be found, tree-like.

A visit to Madeira, for most plant lovers, may well involve an excursion to the Botanical Gardens. At the time C. T.-S. wrote, it didn't exist as such; otherwise I am sure he would have been a frequent visitor. The Quinta do Bom Sucesso (in which the gardens are to be found today) had been built, but the Botanical Gardens were only opened in 1960. A visit to these gardens in spring gives, from a single source, views of all the indigenous and endemic plants of Madeira; succulents, many from South America; as well as tropical trees and aromatic and medicinal plants from around the world.

*

Not everything found on Madeira blooms, something C. T.-S. appreciated and included in his account of the island. A walk beside any levada or wooded area (and this is where the led walks come into their own, especially if you are fortunate enough to have a knowledgeable guide) will almost certainly result in the discovery of a large variety of fern.

> *The levada on the east side of the Metade Valley ... following its course either westward ... or eastward ... the pedestrian will be rewarded with a view of very luxuriant fern life. Here especially will he note the Killarney fern (Trichomanes radicans) and the filmy ferns (Hymenophyllum Tunbridgense and H. unilaterale). These grow in masses on damp rocks and sometimes clothe the gnarled trunks of the ancient laurels. Here also may be found the curious cow's tongue fern (Acrostichum squamosum) growing in the same manner. I have observed this fern in great profusion, and of unusual size ...*
>
> *At a lower altitude on the north side of the island banks and walls will be found full of Asplenium furcatum growing side by side with the ivy-leaf fern; and on the coast itself the sea spleenwort flourishes everywhere.*
>
> *In all there are about forty species of ferns found in the island; of these three are peculiar to Madeira, and five to the North Atlantic islands ...*
>
> *Some slight knowledge of ferns undoubtedly adds great interest to a country walk. It would almost seem that they have an eye for the picturesque. I have noticed in this and in other countries that the finest ferns are often to be found amid the finest scenery.*

In addition to flowers and ferns, Madeira also has abundant varieties of fruit trees.

> *Among fruits, the banana is always with us, and is much better eating than the travelled specimen we know at home. The custard apple, delicious when at its creamy best in January, is becoming stringy and tasteless now. But the passion-flower fruit – that huge and glorified gooseberry – is ripening, and the loquat, the Japanese quince, is displaying its abundance of golden clusters. If not of universal acceptance raw, it makes very tasty tarts, and a*

jam with few rivals. With its large and shiny dark green foliage it is a handsome tree in itself.

Madeirans seem to have a collective sweet tooth (but then don't we all, although possibly theirs may stem from the days when sugar was central to the Madeiran economy). The need for regular sugar surges sits well with the flourishing coffee and cake culture, something with which most tourists are only too willing to join in. So, let's make time for a brief visit to sample the contents of a local patisserie.

The traditional Madeira cake (a classic recipe for which found its way into Mrs Beeton's *Book of Household Management* of 1861) is unlike anything served on Madeira and makes one wonder how a mildly vanilla-flavoured sponge came to be linked with the island. Instead, you are more likely to be served with a dark honey cake called Bolo de Mel. Especially popular at Christmas, when the shopping aisles are stacked high with pre-parcelled versions, in taste it does have some similarities shared with our traditional Christmas cake (minus the white icing) and can include dried fruit and nuts. If you are lucky enough to find an artisan baker's version, it's not to be passed by.

The Pastéis de nata is the Portuguese version of the custard tart. It is baked and has the proportions and deceptive appearance of a small Yorkshire pudding. It first appeared in the eighteenth century, when monks in Lisbon developed the recipe. It wasn't long before they realised its appeal, enjoying the unexpected revenues it brought. Sprinkled with sugar and cinnamon, they can look slightly overbaked, but don't be deceived. A bite into its custardy interior is sure to win over any doubting Thomas. Fortunately, they are now enjoyed all year round, with a variety of fruit-flavoured variations. It's even arrived in shops in the UK. A café in South Kensington sells nothing but Pastéis de nata, which adds a nice touch to any visit to 'museum land' or the Royal Albert Hall.

Bolo Rei or Twelfth Night cake is another unmistakable seasonal favourite, most notably eaten at the King's Festival in January. It is a traditional Portuguese sweet bread, mixed with nuts and crystallised (candied) fruit. Legend has it that the Three Kings couldn't agree on who should be the first to present their gift to the newborn baby. The story goes that a baker gave them a loaf of bread with a broad bean baked inside, telling them that whichever of them found the bean in their slice of bread should present their gift first. It's a little like the tradition of putting sixpence or a thruppenny bit into the Christmas pudding mix, bringing good luck to the finder. Common sense has prevailed, so these days you are less likely to find anything out of the ordinary inside a slice of Bolo Rei.

If you are looking for something more typically Madeiran, the Bolo Familia or family cake makes good use of honey and spices along with crystallised fruits. Malassadas is a must for anyone fond of doughnuts. Deep-fried and covered in sugar or honey they are especially popular at Carnival. Queijadas, a baked Madeiran cheesecake, also takes some beating.

But that's enough sweet things for the moment, so let's head back to the garden awaiting us in springtime.

*

On any garden island, one might expect to find a large variety of insects and birds. As with the plant life, the quinta tenants were sometimes responsible for trying to introduce new species to the island.

> *Of the more agreeable insects, we are favoured throughout the winter with the presence of the Red Admiral butterfly, and, less commonly, of the Painted Lady ... We have endeavoured to acclimatize his first cousin the Peacock butterfly, by introducing a considerable number in the chrysalis stage, but so far have not seen a specimen of the perfect insect. With the spring comes the lovely Clouded Yellow. I am under the impression that I have observed the Pale Clouded Yellow (Colias Hyale), but I can find no record of its having been noticed by others.*

As for birds, surprisingly few small 'feathered friends' are to be found in the towns. The island is, of course, away from the normal bird migration routes, with most visiting birds arriving having been blown off course. Perhaps the reduction in natural open spaces has also had some effect, in depriving them of their usual habitat.

Away from the developed areas you are more likely to see birds of prey, like the sparrowhawk, kestrel and buzzard, which also seek out the weaker, smaller birds. Seabirds seem to fare much better here.

The absence of birdlife, especially small birds, however, is not a modern phenomenon.

> *Birds are not very numerous in Madeira, perhaps because of the prevalence of the kestrel, which may be seen everywhere in town and country. It will sometimes even snatch the tame canaries from their reed cages as they hang outside the houses. And it is to be feared that, as in France, every feathered thing is game to the peasant with a gun. But at this season, the wild canaries, peculiar to Madeira and the Canary Islands, are building in all our garden trees, and enlivening us with their song. Among other garden friends are the grey wagtail, the linnet, the ring sparrow and the goldfinch. The red-legged partridge, the woodcock and the quail breed in the island ... The snipe is said to be a periodical visitor. Stragglers of various species sometimes arrive from the African coast, especially after the prevalence of a strong east wind; and even American species have been observed, a fact very interesting to naturalists, as it suggests a way in which the seeds of American plants may have reached the island in the past.*

More recently, regularly organised birdwatching trips have been advertised for tourists. Seabirds still tend to dominate, but it's reported that there are now forty-six types of breeding bird known to the island.

*

The earliest settlers on Madeira had the good sense to bring vines with them! So successful was the introduction of the grape to the island that, even from the very earliest times, Madeira was referred to as 'the Island of Wine'. Customs House records from the middle of the seventeenth century show the extent of the export trade, and it was obviously a highly regarded commodity.

> *Mr Yate Johnson quotes from the account of Paterson's disastrous expedition ... in 1698 ... that when his vessel touched at Madeira "those gentlemen who had fine clothes among their baggage were glad to exchange embroidered coats and laced waistcoats for provisions and wine." And John Atkins, a surgeon in the navy, who was here about 1720, relates that he bought a pipe of wine for two half-worn suits, and another pipe for three second-hand wigs.*

However, it was the technique for ageing and improving the wine, known as *estufagem*, developed in the eighteenth century, which created a new marketable export. It had been recognised for some time that wine shipped to the tropics and left on board for several years considerably improved in quality. *Estufas*, built to house the wine and provide a source of heat as it matured, were found to achieve the same results. Madeiran fortified wines became a highly fashionable drink, most especially in England.

An island devoted to winemaking needs flourishing vineyards, and springtime on the island is equally important for the growers and vintners.

> *The vines have all been pruned during February, and are now putting forth their leaves. I have spoken of the wine industry as a declining one, but wine is still in point of value the only important export from the island … The attack of temperance from which the Western world appears to be suffering is producing much distress among those concerned one way or another in the supply of intoxicating drinks …*
>
> *But the wine trade of Madeira has passed through many vicissitudes in the past, and perhaps when the world has recovered from its headache and is athirst again, the rich golden wine without rival of its kind will once more enjoy a vogue.*

Although a much less significant part of the economy than it once was, commercial winemaking still thrives today. The area around Camara de Lobos is the most productive grape-growing area of the island. Millions of litres of the traditional Madeira wines are produced, bearing the cherished "Madeiran Origin" protected status. Of late, some new table wines have also begun to appear. The Madeira Wine Festival takes place in late summer and provides the perfect opportunity for sampling the full range.

Non-commercial vines are also much in evidence. Walking around the small cultivated terraces beside the levadas, even on the edges of Funchal, it is noticeable how many vines are found growing beside private houses. We must assume a unique form of Madeiran 'homebrew' is still very much in vogue here.

As for the other old staple crop, which once formed the backbone of the Madeiran economy, sugar, spring was once a time of great activity on the streets of Funchal, as C. T.-S describes.

This is a busy season in the fazenda, or farm. The sugar-cane is now being cut, and the streets of Funchal are full of ox-drawn sledges conveying bundles of it to the mill. By a curious perversity these are laid cross-wise on the sledge, instead of length-wise, with the result that the ends will sometime strike the legs of the unwary wayfarer, or otherwise obstruct traffic, and much shouting and vituperation is the outcome. A cloud of urchins hovers around the sledges, eager to pilfer a cane as occasion may serve. In this land of abundant cane and dear sugar, youth seldom tastes any other sweetmeat.

Small amounts of sugar cane are still milled in Calheta, Porto da Cruz and Funchal, with visitors welcome to watch the process. Preserved as much for posterity as for production (although it's understood output has recently increased slightly), these working mills also largely supply the domestic demands for sugar cane honey by the bakers of traditional honey cake and *aguardente*, the essential ingredient vital to those poncha sellers looking to satisfy customers with the original genuine article.

The window for processing cane is short. It needs to arrive at the mill within hours of cutting; otherwise the cane becomes dry and useless. This may explain the hive of activity C. T.-S. observed in the centre of Funchal, in the days when many cane mills were to be found in the city.

Today, the only thing likely to obstruct traffic, bringing it to a standstill, is when roads are closed for the more important street processions or road races. Very quickly, the narrow streets of Funchal can become clogged; pollution levels and drivers' temperatures rise as they make valiant attempts to break out of the maze of closed streets. Perhaps, then, this is our modern-day equivalent of a smart slap on the legs from an unwieldy bundle of sugar cane being transported by sledge to the nearest mill.

March. Antiquities.

I have long regarded the chapter 'March – Antiquities' as being something of a curiosity, almost an anomaly. It could have appeared just about anywhere in the book and doesn't follow the normal seasonal sequential account of someone overwintering on Madeira. As a result, it sits a little awkwardly with any of the other chapters. Moreover, as with America, whose history has a similar vintage to that of Madeira, that history is relatively short. A visitor coming to the island expecting to find something approaching ancient history is naturally going to be disappointed. Obviously, no fault can be attached to the islanders. It's not something which can be altered or invented, so one might almost wonder why the chapter was included in the first place.

It is only when one reads the obituary of C. T.-S. that appeared in *The Times* on 8 March 1932, that we begin to have a better understanding of why he felt it warranted inclusion. The obituary writer referred to him as *"A scholarly antiquary"* with a keen interest in archaeology; Chairman of the Council of the Sussex Archaeological Society; and a writer on "antiquarian subjects". With that additional information, for someone confessing to pen *"inconsequent ... irrelevant jottings on many subjects"*, it's not altogether surprising that antiquities found their way onto the list of subjects for inclusion. Nevertheless, C. T.-S. recognised the inherent difficulties the chapter presented from the outset.

> *It must be owned that while what we especially enjoy in Madeira – climate, scenery, vegetation – is of surpassing excellence, many things are lacking ... We have to go without all the romance which springs from that suggestion of ancient civilizations which is everywhere present in Mediterranean countries. The chance of turning up even a Corinthian stater amid our sugar canes would invest spadework with a new interest. And our gardens lack that spice of immemorial antiquity which is added in Italy by the presence of a broken column, or a battered bust; which even in many English gardens proceeds from the proximity of an ancient church, a fragment of a city wall, or a castle shattered in the civil wars.*

> *"I sometimes think that never blows so red*
> *The Rose as were some buried Caesar bled;*
> *That every Hyacinth the Garden wears*
> *Dropt in its Lap from some once lovely Head."*

> *It seems an undoubted fact that previous to the Portuguese colonization this island was uninhabited. No vestiges of any previous race, civilized or uncivilized, have ever come to light. It may have been visited by early explorers ... But even if it was visited, it was not settled, and we are therefore denied all the sentimental excitement and the practical labour of searching for antiquities.*

> *If the Romans had not shrunk from exploration on the high seas – a curious want of enterprise considering their taste for conquest and colonization: and in the course of their wanderings had occupied Madeira, our gain would perhaps be not merely that of the antiquary and scholar, but practical. Roads, bridges, aqueducts, and other public works would surely have survived the fall of the Empire, and as elsewhere within its confines would either serve modern uses, or point the way for their successors.*

> *And a very little thing turned the scale and left this fertile island unoccupied for another fifteen hundred years.*

While Madeira may not have an excessively long history of habitation, it does – of course – share a common culture with Portugal, which most certainly does. Whether there were earlier attempts to settle on the island or just sightings, it is always possible the task of clearing the island, making it fit for occupation, proved too daunting.

> *It is related by the old chroniclers that when the island was discovered it was clothed with dense woods. To clear it for cultivation they were set fire to. The conflagration is said to have lasted ten years, and on one occasion to have mastered the colonists and driven them to their ships. This story is probably only a poetic way of saying that it took ten years to destroy the primeval vegetation on the ground required for the cultivation of sugar-cane; and it is quite possible that man's needs in more recent times have had as much to do with extinction of the native flora as this possibly mythical fire.*

Madeira's near neighbours, the Canary Islands, have had a very different history.

> Lying as they do much nearer to the coast of Africa, and their loftiest peak being of such a soaring height, they could not escape the notice of the early voyagers who passed from the Mediterranean to the Atlantic and skirted the Libyan coast in their southward course. And they therefore seem to have been fairly well known to the ancients. When, at the close of the Crusades, the adventurers of Western Europe turned their attention to the Atlantic, these islands were inhabited by a semi-civilized people, possibly of Egyptian origin, as they practised the mummification of their dead ... These islanders made a very gallant defence of their country against the invading Spaniards, and from the date of the Jean de Bethencourt's expedition to conquer them in 1402 a century elapsed before they were completely subdued. It must be owned that in the stirring details of this conquest, and in the relics of these mysterious and interesting people, the Canaries possess an asset which Madeira with its more peaceful history lacks.

The earliest constructions on Madeira took place in the fifteenth century, with fortification of Funchal and its bay taking place at the beginning of the sixteenth century.

The foundations of a section of the old sixteenth-century city wall were unearthed following the 2010 floods, and after careful excavation its archaeological footprint can now be seen just below the marketplace at Praça da Autonomia, near to where the two rivers (Santa Luzia and João Gomes) make acquaintance with the sea. It was here that the Fort of São Filipe once stood, built over in the early twentieth century to house a sugar factory. Sadly, the needs of industry at the time outweighed any thoughts of conservation or heritage.

The factory was destroyed by fire and thereafter began a slow process of uncovering more of the ruins of the old fortifications. Fortunately, the original plans survived, and a raised walkway now allows pedestrians to look down on the unearthed ruins and imagine city life many centuries ago.

That it should have been the sugar industry which overshadowed the preservation of a historical structure is possibly more significant than might at first be thought. It was sugar which had the greatest impact not just in the development of Madeira, but in the island's influence on Western civilisation.

> Although Madeira has played no great part in human story, and has no imposing relics of the past to show, it was nevertheless the nursery of two

> *very notable things, which profoundly influenced the history of subsequently discovered and colonized Western countries. I have mentioned that its colonization was the first step in that world-wide Portuguese over-sea enterprise which blazed up in the succeeding century, and led the Pope to divide the new world between Portugal and Spain. Into Madeira Prince Henry introduced some shoots of sugar-cane from Sicily, and here he organized the first cultivation and manufacture of sugar on a large scale, and from Madeira the cultivation spread to the West Indies when they were discovered and settled. The deficiency of white labour for the working of this crop led to the importation into Madeira of large numbers of negroes from Africa, their first employment by Europeans in the development of a new country, and a step which later led to very momentous consequences in North and South America. For hence arose "that execrable sum of all villanies", the slave trade.*

With the decline in the sugar trade during the sixteenth century (due to competition from Brazil and the Spanish colonies of South America), a replacement was found, firstly in wine and, much more recently, in tourism.

Despite the lack of antiquities, for the tourist, there is much to admire on Madeira, although architecture is probably not foremost in any tourist's mind.

> *Although the general aspect of Funchal may be described as "old-world", yet it suggests rather the comfortable and leisurely world of the eighteenth century than anything earlier. An old house or two with a sixteenth-century coat-of-arms and date may be seen; some of the churches were built not long after the original occupation, but they contain very little of interest. The cathedral, which was finished in 1514, is not an interesting building as a whole; but its ceiling of juniper wood, commonly said to be Moorish in character, and distantly recalling some Venetian work of the period, is very fine. The sacristy contains a good deal of elaborate carving of the sixteenth century, and a number of pictures which to describe as of no merit is too mild. The Church of the Convent of Sta. Clara, in which Zargo, the first governor, is buried, is lined with very beautiful tiles with an interlaced arabesque design, I think, of early sixteenth-century work, and the effect is most pleasing; but there is little in the whole town which one would take the trouble to look at in Italy or Spain. None of the fine arts seem to have flourished here at any time ...*

> *In masonry the good Latin tradition of sound and substantial work still survives, and the houses are built with great solidity. One misses the stone stairways and marble balustrades of Italy, but pleasant fountains and stone seats of passably good design are common; and long pergolas with stone pillars and tops of chestnut wood are an agreeable feature. The houses were formally roofed with brown-grey tiles which "weather" to a very charming and reposeful tint. These were unfortunately abandoned some years ago for tiles of that staring red which one sees in the neighbourhood of Marseilles; and more recently a hideous diaper design of many colours has come into fashion. And architectural taste generally is at present at a very low ebb.*

If Madeira has, through no fault of its own, scant offerings of an archaeological nature, what about furniture and precious metals? At the time in which C. T.-S. wrote, here the signs were certainly brighter.

> *The collector – we are all collectors nowadays – who cares for English furniture and silver of the eighteenth century, has sometimes found Madeira a happy hunting-ground. In house after house – English and Portuguese – you may see good old English furniture, especially fine chairs and settees, some undoubtedly the work of the great English makers; while others are local copies and adaptations of their designs. And as the Madeira cabinet makers have always been masters of their craft, the latter are not to be despised. They may generally be detected by the great heaviness of the island mahogany from which they are made, and by their missing in some indefinable way the quality which genius impresses. But the real thing is not uncommon.*

Today, Funchal, and therefore Madeira, is not awash with antique shops, so if this is your passion, then like archaeological 'finds', you may be disappointed. The quality furniture, of which C. T.-S. speaks, is generally treasured in private houses, including some of the more distinguished quinta hotels, another reason for visiting these old country houses. A hundred years ago, however, antique good-quality furniture and household items would have been more regularly available to buy.

> *Strangers often express surprise at this abundance of old English furniture in a foreign country. It is explained by the fact that in the seventeenth and especially in the eighteenth centuries many Englishmen settled here to exploit the wine trade; they made a great deal of money, and built themselves fine houses, and sent to England for their furniture and plate. And as later the East Indiamen commonly called here for wine, Madeira probably had more*

> regular communication with England than even with Portugal. There is, however, a persistent tradition that Thomas Chippendale himself at one time resided and worked either in Portugal or here. I can find no authority for this, but the surprising amount of work more or less showing his influence seems to lend some colour to the story, which is not in itself incredible.
>
> It is not to be supposed that you can walk into a shop and buy such treasures. The getting of them still has some of the excitement of the hunt. There are as yet no dealers in curios, and there are consequently no sham antiquities at genuine prices.

The East Indiamen and the settlers were not alone in bringing furniture and plate to the island. Many of the marketable treasures also belonged to the quinta tenants. At the end of a period of stay, quinta residents were occasionally known to sell personal items brought with them, to pay for rent due or bills outstanding. To get the best price, one can assume that the 'grapevine' was well used to generate as much interest as possible, and bargains were to be had.

> Occasionally an old piece finds its way to one of the cabinet makers, or if it is known that you are looking out for such things you hear of them ... Everything is known everywhere at once ... And when you do get a chance of buying, you are generally asked quite old-fashioned prices. I bought a "Chippendale" chair for twenty-two shillings. It was covered with green paint; this being washed off it stood revealed as of the finest design and workmanship. And do we not possess one of the most beautiful silver cake-baskets ever seen, with London mark and date 1762, which was bought for a trifle more than its weight in dollars?
>
> Occasionally the contents of an old house are sold by auction. If the sale occurs during the winter season, when the town is full, fair prices may be obtained for the more obviously attractive lots. But great bargains are sometimes to be had.

For present-day bargain hunters, the grapevine may still exist among the more permanent residents. For everyone else, there are just a very few antique shops we have found in the area just north of the La Vie shopping centre, on Rua da Mouraria and not far from the English Church. Although I am by no means an expert in such things, they give one the impression of selling memorabilia, although some pieces of furniture are available.

While Madeira may lack anything approaching antiquities in the true sense, today there is nevertheless a keen attention paid to preserving reminders of its historic past, for the benefit of tourists.

This book began by rejecting any notion that it should be regarded as a tourist's guide. But in one slight departure, here is a list of some of the museums and tourist attractions offering insights into a range of historical and contemporary life on the island:

> *The Story Centre Museum, Funchal.* A useful starting point. Located near to the cable car station, this museum traces the island's history from volcanic eruption, through to discovery, and up to the present day.
>
> *Blandy's Wine Lodge, Funchal.* The Blandy family have been producing Madeira wine on the island for more than 200 years. The Lodge (located on Avenida Arriaga near to the Ritz Café) offers the chance to discover the history of madeira winemaking.
>
> *Madeira Embroidery Museum IBTAM, Funchal.* Located on Rua Visconde de Anadia, this museum contains the finest collection of embroideries and tapestries from the island in the nineteenth and twentieth centuries.
>
> *Palácio de São Lourenço, Funchal.* This unmistakable landmark on the waterfront is a sixteenth-century fort, once the home of the island's governors and military. Restored in 1943, it now houses the Military Museum.
>
> *Funchal Municipal Museum of Natural History and Aquarium, Funchal.* This museum has a collection of Madeira's natural history of flora, fauna and marine life. The museum is in Rua da Mouraria in the Palace of São Pedro.
>
> *Frederico de Freitas House Museum, Funchal.* This museum, also known as the Casa de Calçada, was once the home of Dr Frederico de Freitas (1894–1978), who spent nearly forty years bringing together a stunning collection of works of art, later bequeathed to Madeira.
>
> *Museu de Electricidade, Funchal.* The Museum of Electricity offers a display of rare machinery and equipment from over a century.

Museu do Brinquedo, Funchal. Opened in 2003, the Toy Museum hosts twelve thousand exhibits including antique toys, such as miniature cars, aeroplanes, dolls, toy soldiers and many more. If you wish to relive your childhood, you will find the museum located on Rua da Levada dos Barreiros in Funchal.

Museu Arte Sacra, Funchal. The museum of sacred art is housed in a former Bishop's Palace and includes a collection of antique jewellery, sculptures and Flemish paintings from the fifteenth to the eighteenth century.

Mário Barbeito de Vasconcelos Library-Museum, Funchal. You will find this museum located on Avenida Arriaga. It features a rare collection of ancient books, coins, maps and charts left behind by Christopher Columbus, dating back to the sixteenth century, including articles about Madeira's history.

Sugar Museum, Funchal. This museum was once the home of João Esmeraldo, a Flemish settler and merchant who traded sugar between Madeira and Europe. The exhibition traces the history of sugar in Madeira, and the importance of sugar to the history and early years, up to the modern-day. The Museum is on Praça do Colombo.

The Whale Museum, Caniçal. A drive east to Caniçal is required to the small fishing village which houses a new museum dedicated to the history of whale hunting in Madeira. Now an extinct industry, the museum looks at hunting methods used, and includes artwork from whalebones and teeth. This modern building, with interactive displays and videos, is an ideal place for all the family to while away half a day at least.

Vicente's Photography Museum, Rua da Carreira, Funchal. Recently reopened after a five-year closure and major redevelopment. The studio was established in 1848 by Vicente Gomes da Silva and later transformed into a museum, housing hundreds of photographs plotting the island's past heritage.

March. The North Side.

A journey to the north side of this island is something quite apart from the ordinary run of travel in the modern world. A very mountainous country girt with precipitous sea-cliffs and intersected by a succession of ravines; with no roads other than mere horse-tracks at the best and almost impassable foot-paths at the worst; an absence of any other than the most simple lodging and most homely fare in the seldom visited villages; such are the conditions of the journey. But its very difficulties have produced their own remedy. The necessity of carrying across mountain passes or up precipitous cliffs everything not locally produced has bred a race of porters unsurpassed for strength and endurance in the world, porters who take a very pride in the weight of their loads, who will delight to carry not only your luggage but yourself, who will make shift to carry your grand piano if you have a fancy to take it with you. Wherefore it is possible for the modest traveller who is content with a change of clothes, and some certainty of provision in the shape of a tinned tongue and a little tea, who will ride or walk as occasion serves, and if he or she knocks up be content to be borne in a hammock by casual peasants – they are all porters more or less – it is possible for such an one to journey with a light heart and a single attendant. The less hardy may think a second bearer for a camp bed and some blankets not out of place; the sybarite who wants more had better stick to the hotels and casino of Funchal.

Today's traveller will find that transportation around the island is considerably less daunting. The experience of being carried over hills and mountains, by hammock or palanquin, has eluded this writer, as it has visitors for many years. To be able to savour, from a seated or lying down position, the breathtaking views around every bend and turn, without putting any effort into getting there, just sounds too good to be true. Accounts of those who made use of these forms of transport, however, suggest they may not have been quite as imagined. Suspended about twelve inches above the ground, they were said to be cramped, with the possibility of being jolted against some protruding rock or bush an ever-present and unsettling threat.

Car hire offers a far simpler way of exploring the island's coastal regions today. With a shoreline of about 88 miles, you might think one circular lap is doable in a day, but it would mean missing so much. Where time permits, and at the right season of the year, if the opportunity for an excursion to one or other of the coastal areas presents itself, the chance should not be missed. C. T.-S. chose to explore the north side on one of his frequent visits to the island.

At the north-east corner lies the town of Santana, a frequent starting point for an exploration of the north coastline. It is also where many tourists come to see the traditional Madeiran houses, with their pitched roofs extending to ground level. Travelling there today makes good use of the Rapide motorways and tunnels (including the longest tunnel on the island, stretching for a little over three kilometres).

The entire northern coast, from east to west, leads through the towns of São Jorge, Boaventura, Ponta Delgada, São Vicente, Seixal and, finally, Porto Moniz. The Rapide makes light work of the whole of the northern coastline. It would be so easy to describe this journey from the comfy interior of a car, coach or minibus, but how much more thrilling to make an imaginary journey, on foot or horseback, as C. T.-S. did over a hundred years ago.

So, let's take the opportunity afforded by his writing, accepting the invitation to ride this same rugged terrain, astride a pony of twelve hands, with bulging overnight saddlebags strapped in place, and several heavily laden attendants ready to guide us on the way. It's an opportunity to explore a great wilderness, far removed from any of the comforts and conveniences of twenty-first-century life. An unforgettable and unique journey, with saddle-sores an entirely imaginary threat.

But first, we must travel from Funchal to Santana, before embarking out along the length of the north coast.

> *The roads or tracks which cross the central range of mountains radiate from Funchal like the sticks of a fan. They all lead the traveller through mountain and sylvan scenery of great beauty, especially on the northern watershed.*
>
> *I have already described the chief route across the island so far as Ribeiro Frio, the excursion which gives to many visitors their one glimpse of the northern valleys. The traveller who instead of returning to Funchal pursues this route to the village of Sta. Anna [Santana] will pass through a succession of enchanting scenes, "an intermingled pomp of hill and vale". He will ascend ridge after ridge and descend into valley after valley, each*

> *differing from each in character, yet now and then displaying that curious repetition of feature, that suggestion of imitative power, which are sometimes very marked in the scenery of volcanic mountains. Perhaps the finest part of the route is where the traveller crosses the Metade valley ... Looking back, he gazes once more into the stupendous recesses of the great ravine; the view if less intimate is more mysterious; and if clouds have gathered on the crests and hide the topmost crags of Arriero and the Torres, their lower cliffs will appear the more appalling for the gloom above. At this season the lower hills are made glorious by the common broom, "flooding the mountain-sides for miles with seas of golden blossoms" ... In some places the broom is being completely superseded by the common gorse, which was introduced about one hundred years ago, and has spread over the whole island ...*
>
> *Passing from the slopes of the lower hills, the traveller enters a sylvan region, and emerges from it to arrive at the pleasant village of Sta. Anna. Here are masses of hydrangeas, which must be glorious in summer, and the hedges are full of fuchsias and other flowering plants. At this season the air is still fresh and keen, for Sta. Anna lies at an elevation of eleven or twelve hundred feet.*

We have visited Santana on several occasions and have seen it in many guises, probably the most beguiling of which was at Carnival. The Island's 'Festas de Carnaval' lasts a little over a week and begins in this north-eastern corner of the island, at Santana, with the Compadres Parade.

'Compadres' are chosen by a child's parents at christening and confirmation, and also by the bride and groom at weddings (they perform similar duties to godparents, the best man and bridesmaids). This parade celebrates the good and the bad, recognising the arduous responsibilities accompanying the role, which should not be taken lightly. Stuffed images of compadres, left hanging by the neck from lampposts, send out a dire warning to those who do not live up to expectations. Despite this slightly sinister, surreal backdrop, it gets the Carnival season off to a lively and entertaining start.

Santana is an ideal place to begin exploring the north coast.

> *Using Sta. Anna [Santana] as a centre, the traveller may explore much of the northern coast; he may ascend the six thousand feet to Ruivo, the highest summit of the island, or, by means of the levadas which tap their streams, he may find his way into the great valleys and their ramifications which*

> extend deep into the central range. The village itself lies a short distance from the edge of the sea-cliffs, which are here about one thousand feet high and rich in all the elements of savage grandeur.
>
> Here he may look down on little coves and isolated beaches, such as Stevenson would have loved to endow with the romance of a piratical past, and he may dream of days when perchance they were put to nefarious, if picturesque, uses. In some of its features ... solitary and peaked rocks stand out in the sea, and ceaseless fret of the waves has in more than one instance worn a passage through the centre of such a rock, forming a natural arch.

So, we're about ready to depart. But there's one last thing to do: let's take the opportunity to see the neighbouring island of Porto Santo, visible on a good day from Santana.

> As one looks northwards across the ocean, the island of Porto Santo is ever a prominent object, hanging like a fairy isle between the sea and the sky. It is but six miles long, with an extreme width of three miles ... Its loftiest peak is about 1660 feet high. There are no trees, and from a distance it affords a strangely barren contrast to the fertile aspect of Madeira. It is a poor little place, with a mail only every two or three weeks, when the weather permits a small steamer to make the voyage from Funchal: and life on the island must be the dullest.

The daily ferry service (no longer a small steamer but a ro-ro car carrier) and an airport must at least have made living on Porto Santo less isolated. In winter months, the weather still has the habit of disrupting these daily sailings. Unlike Madeira, the beaches on Porto Santo are of yellow sand, and it's a place that comes into its own in the summer months.

Having now viewed Porto Santo, albeit from a distance, it's time to climb into our theoretical saddle once more, with a long day's ride ahead of us, westwards. C. T.-S. takes up the account.

> Delightful as is the vicinity of Sta. Anna, the traveller who wishes to realize fully the beauty and grandeur of the north coast must travel further westward. In the course of his journey he will descend into the ravines of many rivers, crossing them perhaps not much above sea-level, and ascend again and again by tortuous and steep paths the ridges which divide them. These wanderings will lead him along the face of headlands, against the base

> of which, perhaps a thousand or fifteen hundred feet directly below, the surf thunders unceasingly. In such awe-inspiring situations, along a rough and narrow path hewn in the rock, he may perhaps deem it wiser to lead his horse than to ride him. And the grandest and wildest path of all can only be traversed on foot.
>
> West of Sta. Anna lies the village of St Jorge, situate also about a thousand feet above the sea. It looks but a little way off ... From a point on the cliffs below the village the long line of surf-beaten cliffs may be seen in all their glory ... the traveller may ride in another three hours to Boa Ventura, passing on the journey one of those fearful headlands which I have described.
>
> Where every prospect pleases, where you may make your choice between beetling crags and sylvan gorges, and flowery meads and sea-sprayed cliffs, it is difficult to select one spot on this northern shore as more truly delightful than another. Yet, if I must make a choice, I do not hesitate to choose the village of Boa Ventura, of "Good Fortune", as the very gem. The hamlet lies some 1400 feet above the sea-level, on a spur of mountain standing out into one of the main valleys of the island, perhaps the most glorious of all its valleys ...
>
> The Portuguese seem to have, consciously or unconsciously, a happy knack of selecting a fine and romantic position for the last resting-place of their dead ... the rude forefathers of Boa Ventura sleep amid a scene of beauty not easily matched. To sit in the evening hour by the churchyard wall and watch the shadows creeping upwards from the already dark valleys towards the reddening peaks, while far below the Atlantic rollers break and spirt in spume through the honeycombed reefs; to note how the last lingering rays of the setting sun illumine the graves of the unnamed dead; such is an experience not readily forgotten.

Today, we tend to measure distances in miles or kilometres, but C. T.-S. (like all travellers at this time) was more familiar with estimating the length of time it would take to get from one place to another, whether on horseback or on foot. So far, we have travelled from Santana to Boaventura (via São Jorge). A car might expect to cover that distance in less than thirty minutes. The distance table included in the 1851 publication *Madeira, its Climate and Scenery* suggests a duration of a little over six hours for the same journey. A long time to be in the saddle and, given the description of descending twilight, it would almost certainly have been time to consider setting up camp for the night: the horses tended to; tents erected; a meal cooked on an open fire; and with twilight fading to the rhythmic motion of the Atlantic rollers on the beach below, it's time to turn in for the night. Tomorrow will be another long day, with a detour to see the northern view of the Curral das Freiras, all of which calls for an early start. So, perhaps taking the opportunity for one last look upwards at the star-filled sky; the fire embers dampened; we creep under canvas, wrapping ourselves in the various rugs and blankets brought for the purpose. Once comfortable, we bid the day adieu.

> *From the village of Boa Ventura a path leads up the valley and over a high mountain-pass, called the Torrinhas, to the southern side and Funchal. This path, if in good order, is perhaps just passable for horses; if landslips have occurred to damage it, it may be, as I once chanced to find it, scarcely passable on foot. From the village it descends a few hundred feet to the level of the little river, which in a more northern land would make an ideal trout stream. By the side of this it ascends for some miles, passing gradually from the cultivated lands to the region of primeval forest, the enclosing walls of rock becoming ever grander as we bore deeper into the mass of the central range. At length we appear to reach an impasse. The valley at its head widens into a circular amphitheatre, suggesting an extinct volcano, without reason, as the geologists tell us. The scene offers an unsurpassed combination of the stupendous and the picturesque. The mountain-sides are clothed with forest ... Looking upwards through their branches, we catch glimpses of the crags and pinnacles above ... Up one of the slopes our path finds a way of interminable zigzags till we reach the level of the pass, nearly five thousand feet above the sea. A comparatively level stretch bordered here and there by great smooth rocks of unusual form and affording views of the vale below, which fill us with awe and admiration, leads to the Torrinhas Pass itself. We hasten through a narrow opening in the jagged summit, and a different world lies at our feet. We are at the head of the greatest valley of the southern side, the Curral das Freiras, known to the tourists who visit its lower end from Funchal as the Grand Curral; and beyond it stretches the Southern ocean ...*

> *The enterprising traveller will prefer to return to Boa Ventura and to continue his exploration of the north coast, of which the wildest portion still awaits him. In a few hours' ride from the fair village, which he will no doubt have left with regret, he will reach the little town of S. Vicente, lying at the narrow mouth of one of the grandest of the island's valleys.*

At this point, many modern-day tourists will choose to pause and explore the caves at São Vicente. In referring to them as 'caves', one might immediately imagine vast sea-cliff-faced caverns, smugglers and hidden booty. Instead, however, one encounters caves of a totally different kind: a labyrinth of unique lava flow tubes, some as much as a kilometre in length. They were discovered at about the same time C. T.-S. first visited the island, although not opened to the public until 1996.

They give a dramatic illustration of lava's journey from the core of the eruption, such as would have occurred at the time the island came into existence over five million years ago. Excavated in the 1880s, these arterial volcanic veins were once filled with a mixture of red-hot lava and gas. As the outer layers cooled and solidified, setting like some straitjacket skin, the excess lava continued to flow deep within the tubes, escaping wherever a crack in the earth's surface allowed it to flow.

> *This island stands six thousand feet high, amid sea-depths more than twice as great. It has been piled up on the ocean's bed by a series of eruptions repeated again and again, sometimes in rapid succession, sometimes at long intervals, over a period of time to be reckoned by tens of thousands of years. Earthquakes have riven the layers of solid rock and filled the fissures with lava, now to be seen in the form of dykes intersecting the highest hills To earthquakes are due the vast rendings of the rock which through the subsequent action of the elements have become those "trenches of the long-drawn vales" that delight us today. Everywhere, in highland and lowland alike, we behold traces of a prolonged and appalling volcanic activity. For many centuries it has been stilled, and we who dwell upon its slumbering ashes may dare to hope that the forces which gave it birth will rest for ever contented with their labour.*

Within these tubes are to be found the now cooled lava. It has the appearance of a smooth riverbed, but only the eyes are deceived. To the touch, it has an abrasive character more like razor-sharp coral.

The inside of the caves is warmer than might be expected and, with only artificial light, a night's beard's growth of greenery occasionally manages to cling to the wall's damp surface. The germinating seeds will have been carried there most likely on visitors' clothing or in air spores. The constant irrigating drip, drip, from the cavern roof ensures a regular supply of fresh water. The moisture, temperature and light are more than enough to maintain this tiny form of plant life deep underground.

The literature advertising the caves describes them as a journey to the centre of the earth, which possibly over-eggs the pudding, but it's a unique experience and worth a pause in one's journey.

> *From S. Vicente westwards a very remarkable path, only passable on foot, has been hewn in the face of the precipitous cliffs. It leads in about two hours to the village of Seixal. It is never more than six feet wide and often much less, it has no parapet, and the overhanging rock sometimes makes it impossible for a tall man to walk upright. Here and there, where waterfalls descend from the hills above, the rock is tunnelled to afford protection. Sometimes the path descends to the sea-level, only to ascend again several hundred feet. And always the cliffs are sheer, with the wild sea breaking at their base. It is not a path suited to the nervous. Wild gullies, deep gashes severing the line of cliff and extending far into the heart of the mountains, are passed on the way. The deepest and most precipitous is called, not inappropriately, Ribeiro do Inferno. The botanist will remark that the moist crannies in the rocks are everywhere filled with splendid specimens of the sea spleenwort, Asplenium marinum; and the cliffs are studded, as elsewhere on the north coast, with a species of houseleek, Sempervivum glandulosum, varying in size from that of a small pincushion to that of the crown of a tall hat, or larger.*

The route between São Vicente and Seixal has some of the most dramatic stretches of coast road anywhere on the island and includes the Bride's Veil waterfall. It is also here that sections of the original coast road can often still be seen, perilously clinging like lichen to the sheer cliff face.

Several years ago, on perhaps our second or third visit to the island, we hired a car, venturing off the Rapide to ride along one of these mere cut-out ledges. With looming cliff walls to one side and steep drops into the sea to the other, warning signs made it quite clear that falling rocks were a distinct possibility, with no one vouching for our safety. It's an opportunity which is now lost, other than for the reckless or foolhardy.

Today, a section of this same road hangs abruptly in mid-air, like the chute of some giant helter-skelter ride, cut short of its ultimate destination. The rest of the road has fallen into the sea, leaving a ragged, almost dissected and jagged edge of tarmac, suspended from the cliff face. Unfortunately, the road was not the only thing to succumb to erosion. We passed by a stretch of ground, running from hilltop, nearly to the sea, looking slightly out of place, almost like a newly planted stretch of garden, yet to be worked. This whole area had once been a part of the village, but a landslide had removed houses and people. Instead of rebuilding, they had decided to leave the area as a natural environmental monument to those who had lost so much.

Reaching Seixal brought C. T.-S.'s journey to an equally abrupt end. As we are about to read, there were no passable roads or paths he could use.

> *At Seixal this unique path comes to an end. Sheer cliffs of great height bar all further passage along the coast, and the traveller bent on proceeding westward must either take boat or ascend to the mountain plateau above.*

A Rapide tunnel gives us the road access denied to C. T.-S. Porto Moniz is the furthest north-western point of the island. Its rock pools, sheltered from the Atlantic rollers, are found more inviting in summer months than in March. Picturesque, wild and naturally beautiful, they offer a unique variation for those fond of sea dipping.

Visitors returning from Porto Moniz to Funchal will find the temptation is to retrace one's steps, along the same Rapide motorways, probably as far as São Vicente and then turning inland to cross the island via the Serra d'Agua valley. This certainly offers the fastest return route and some very impressive views.

If possible, however, why not try something different? The alternative is to return to Funchal along the rooftop of Madeira and the Paul da Serra range, a plateau with unimaginable views of both the north and south coasts of the island. We don't know what route C. T.-S. took in returning to Funchal, but from this extract it wouldn't surprise me to learn that, at some stage, he too had similar thoughts.

> *It is possible [to return] ... by a very rough path up the west side of the vale of Seixal, a valley seldom visited, but almost unrivalled in wealth of vegetation and wild rocky scenery. Above this gorge lies a lovely sylvan and park-like tract with scattered timber, across which a path may be followed to the far-famed waterfalls of Rabacal, whence one of the little ports on the south coast may be reached.*

For the prolonged exploration of the high land in the centre of the island, and the heads of the great ravines, the weather in winter is often unsuitable. But in summer tent life at this altitude must be very delightful.

The wide-open heathland of the central plateau covers about twenty-four square kilometres and is at a height of fifteen hundred metres. The clouds have a habit of rationing the view but, not unlike Snowdonia, a brief clear interlude will often open suddenly and without warning. When it occurs, breath-taking photographic opportunities invariably result. This road across the plateau is narrow and good but not fast. It's a route which invites you to disregard time, and to savour the experience.

*

Perhaps the difficulty in reaching, and then exploring the north side of Madeira, at the start of the twentieth century, presented such challenges as to warrant a separate chapter to itself. This was no afternoon picnic, more an expedition, requiring detailed preparation, which he later described as *"elaborate"* and *"prolonged"*.

Today, we have little opportunity for such extreme ventures, whether on Madeira or anywhere else. Given the ease of travel, the north side is as accessible as any other part of the island. Many excursions to the other coastal regions are available throughout the year, and a trip to the Tourist Information Office or one of the many tour operators will reveal what aspects of coastal life on Madeira hold greatest interest.

The south-east coast, and the São Lourenço peninsula, is a stand-out favourite, whether as part of an organised tour/walk or an itinerary made for oneself. The views are strongly reminiscent of certain areas in the UK. Imagine the Needles on the Isle of Wight, the Gower's Worm's Head or Cornwall's Land's End, and you begin to envisage what is in store.

Depending on the direction of the wind, you might find yourself under the path of the comings and goings from the airport; however, their frequency is never enough to spoil either the occasion or the place. On windy days, it is easy to appreciate the tricky approach aircraft must make when landing here, and why crosswinds can easily disrupt or close the airport. When that happens, passengers can sometimes find themselves landing in Porto Santo, the Canaries or on the mainland instead.

The southern coastline, west of Funchal, never seems to get as many visitors as the other coastal regions. Camara de Lobos and the high cliffs of Cabo Girão, with its glass skywalk suspended out over the cliff edge, giving uninterrupted views of the sea some 500 metres below, are about as far south-west as many visitors travel in that direction.

A trip further westward, however, provides an introduction to one of the few 'yellow' sandy beaches to be found on Madeira. Calheta is an altogether more tranquil and restful resort. The sand is not natural to the resort, of course, and is in marked contrast to the natural black volcanic beach sand elsewhere. Most of this coastline also has precipitous cliffs with roaring Atlantic breakers pounding the rocks, which makes it popular with surfers. They gravitate around Ponta Pequena and Pacel do Mar, although Faja da Areia on the north shore also gets a good deal of surf lovers' attention.

C. T.-S. began his account of the journey to the north side by quoting from the Victorian poet Matthew Arnold. The words catch the mood of everything of which he went in search – and found – making it an equally appropriate epilogue.

> *"And there*
> *The sunshine in the happy glens is fair,*
> *And by the sea, and in the brakes*
> *The grass is cool, the seaside air*
> *Buoyant and fresh, the mountain flowers*
> *More virginal and sweet than ours."*
> *Matthew Arnold 1822–1888*

April. Holy-days and Holidays.

In most western countries, the influence of the Christian Church (of all denominations) has noticeably declined. Weakened and less secure, its authority occasionally undermined by its past, coupled with the imposing busyness of everyday life. All of this is in marked contrast to the position of the church at the beginning of the twentieth century. C. T.-S. gives us a clear and unambiguous view of the Church on the island, about one hundred years ago.

> *The ancient church is here still vigorous and dominant; she is a real force deeply influencing the lives of the people ... And at the evening hour, when the town is already in shadow, but the sunlight still lingers on the hill, and the "Angelus" rings from the tile-clad Campanile, you may indeed feel that here, if anywhere, the Church is still "whispering from her towers the last enchantments of the Middle Ages."*

So, how does the church fare in Madeira today? Is it still *"vigorous and dominant"*, *"deeply influencing"* the lives of the people, or has its sway declined here too?

If church attendance is a good yardstick, then among the older and middle-aged it has the look of reasonable, if maybe not robust, health. Standing outside the cathedral, or Collegiate Church, when services are held, a sizeable congregation attends. Admittedly, not as crowded as at the main religious festivals, but enough to suggest a discernible deep-rooted cultural heartbeat still pumping away.

On Sundays, given Madeira's climate, the doors are often wide open, and the sounds from within hang on the air like the light-wash of a low incense cloud. These sounds are as familiar today as they were to C. T.-S., wherever he went, as this passage illustrates from an excursion made to Boaventura.

> *And it may be that as you stroll back along the level path ... the tower of Santa Quitéria will ring forth the Angelus, telling once more, as it has told through the centuries, its message of peace and consolation.*

As we sat outside Funchal's cathedral today, enjoying the late afternoon sunshine, a middle-aged lady passed by. She drew level just as the chords of a familiar refrain from the choir drifted from the portals. It may even have been the Angelus. She hadn't come from the cathedral, but was just passing, perhaps on her way home. Even the usual city background noise was suddenly temporarily hushed as if a reverential silence was being observed, amplifying the sounds from within. As the congregation began their response, she joined in, keeping perfect harmony. It was a magical moment, and one we felt almost privileged to share. It was over in a second or two, then she was gone, out of earshot of the rest of the service, and unaware we had registered her simple act of participation.

If attendance at religious worship has declined here, as undoubtedly it has (most especially in the capital), then given its past roots, you feel there may still be a deep layer in the human psyche in which it survives. Certainly, this wouldn't have surprised C. T.-S., who began this chapter by quoting from the historian T. B. Macaulay (1800–1859):

> *"She (the Roman Catholic Church) may still exist in undiminished vigour, when some traveller from New Zealand shall, in the midst of a vast solitude, take his stand on a broken arch of London Bridge to sketch the ruins of St Paul's."*

It's a curious quotation, and one which requires some thought. It emphasises the enduring ability of the Roman Catholic church to survive (and with a two-thousand-year history, that's not really open to dispute), even though civilisations and dominions around it rise and ultimately fall. A religion which has outlived the fall of the Roman Empire, and has seen many others come and go, and yet somehow manages to survive. In many ways, it's almost as if religion exists quite independently from its followers. We may support it or turn our back to it, but it is still there. It's a theme which I feel C. T.-S. touched upon again when he wrote of the Church,

> *And she is perhaps the chief sanctuary in Europe of that spiritual side of human nature, which in the intoxication of our material progress we are more and more tending to ignore. Many who have no desire to subscribe to her doctrines, who distrust her dominance, may yet view not without sympathy the greatness of her ideals, the coherence of her ethical system the wholehearted devotion of her servants, her practical wisdom in dealing with*

> *human weakness ... is she not the one unbroken link connecting the civilization of the ancient world and our own?*

A person's attitude to the church is distinctly personal and often varied. Many choose to hold on to those threads of religious fabric which once filled every family living room; others prefer instead to house it in an attic along with other faded family memorabilia; while many more prefer to remove all traces from the house, setting it beyond the garden gate. Whichever, its enduring nature, its ability to survive, even to instil a measure of Catholic guilt, never seems to recede.

Whether the lady we encountered outside the cathedral placed religion in the living room, loft or locked outside the garden fence, we don't know, but those few familiar sounds had clearly resonated deep within her, perhaps reawakening a subconscious memory. Who knows what other thoughts accompanied them. Her response was instinctive, spontaneous and simple, almost devotional. We don't know when she last stepped inside a church. It may have been a week ago or back in her childhood. If the latter, it would go to show religious culture's ability to survive, despite an apparent outward disinterest.

To suggest that attendance at church is as common and consistent today would be unsupportable. Many have lives which are entirely distant and separate from the Church. I would imagine many people only step through church doors to celebrate the main religious festivals, such as Easter and Christmas, much like in the UK.

> *In this still Christian country, Holy Week is not the season of junketing and holiday-making which it has become in England. The Portuguese are by no means inclined to the strict formalism which distinguishes our neo-Catholics. Lent is doubtless a season of fasting and renunciation, though the practice does not appear to be carried to a very irksome degree. But the last days of the Holy Week are universally observed with a rigour and solemnity befitting their associations. The outward sign which strikes the stranger most forcibly is an all-pervading silence. From Thursday to Saturday all sounds are hushed; not a bell rings in church or house; the bells are removed from the very oxen in the street. In a city of bells, religious and secular, among a people which loves and makes noise for its own sake, this has a very solemn and insistent effect. All self-respecting persons are clothed in black, and to the churches unending services and many symbolical representations of the events of the Passion attract throngs of sombre worshipers. Flags are at half-*

> *mast, and the general aspect is the very fitting one of a city mourning for her mighty dead.*
>
> *Yet even during those solemn hours, when on shore all human noise is stilled, when even the roulette at the Casino ceases from spinning, and the decorously impious hide themselves in their houses and play bridge, the traffic of steamers to and from the port knows no cessation. The sanctity of the mail-service surpasses the sanctity of the church; and even the grimy tramp disdains to hush her hideous hooter. Why is the sea thus relieved from the conventions of the land? Why, when the city is actually or officially on its knees in prayer, does Mammon, naked and unashamed, rule the waves? To the faithful such blatant evidence of the triumph of the world must indeed be a stumbling-block and an offence.*
>
> *By a convenient if somewhat illogical arrangement, the week of the Passion ends at the moment of noon on Saturday. The oppressive silence changes suddenly to exuberant noise. The Alleluia is sung in the cathedral; rockets and shells are discharged; and the ringing of bells announces that the long period of mourning is over, and that the joyful celebrations of Easter have commenced.*

A return to the island at Eastertide gave us an opportunity to look for similarities with what C. T.-S. had reported. It would have been very surprising to find that Easter in the island's capital had remained the same: *"universally observed"*; *"an all-pervading silence"*; *"hushed bells"*; *"all self-respecting persons clothed in black"*; *"a city in mourning"*; all are undoubtedly features of a past tradition.

We had not arrived in time to see the formal procession on Palm Sunday, when the Collegiate Church's congregation processed through the streets to the cathedral. On Maundy Thursday, however, Mass was held in an almost full cathedral, and the clergy processed around the cathedral's interior. On Good Friday, a packed Collegiate Church held a vigil during the afternoon, but that apart, much like in the UK, life went on as normal. At noon on Easter Saturday, no bells could be heard, although peals rang from several churches at around sundown, while in the cathedral the congregation sat in a virtually darkened church, keeping vigil.

More obvious signs of seasonal celebration occurred on Easter Sunday, when a procession including bishop, clergy, choir and congregation moved from the cathedral to the founder's statue, watched by an array of tourist cameras.

*

The place of the procession in Madeiran culture goes back a long way.

> *A great feature of the religious life of this as of other Catholic countries is the procession. Processions take place at all seasons, but they are especially used to relieve the monotony of Lent. On March 25, the feast of Our Lady ... of Lourdes ... takes place ... It is composed for the most part of children – the little girls clothed in simple gowns of a violet hue, or of white, with chaplets of natural flowers. Some have wings of gauze, and represent angels. Elder girls, clothed in white as nuns, chant hymns at intervals. Few banners are borne in this procession, the central feature being an image of the Virgin. Behind the long line of children come acolytes in robes of light blue and black, bearing candles; then members of religious confraternities ... and finally, with a bodyguard of stalwart canons, the bowed figure of the good old Bishop in his vestments. The whole affair is a model of order, simplicity and good taste, without a single jarring note.*

> *Pleasant as is the procession itself, a stranger may perhaps be even more impressed by the aspect and behaviour of the crowds which assemble to see it. The line of route is massed with townspeople in gay clothes, and country-folk in their best, the women still for the most part wearing bright shawls, their heads in kerchiefs of different colours, each colour representing to the initiated the parish of their residence ... No police or soldiers are required to keep the line, the people keep it for themselves ... And even when the procession had passed, and a surging mass of humanity filled the roadway, there was no rough horseplay and no undue pushing or scrambling. It was a fine example of give-and-take and self-control.*

Religious processions in the city are certainly not as frequent as they once were. In his book, C. T.-S. lists eleven formal religious processions held in Funchal alone. Aside from the major religious festivals, these will now only occasionally be met.

In February 2016, the pilgrim image of Our Lady of Fatima made a third visit to Madeira. The small icon was received at every one of the island's parishes over a three-week period. Beginning at the Collegiate Church in Funchal, the statue was then transferred to the cathedral by a candle-lit procession, reportedly watched by several thousand onlookers, with Mass held in celebration on arrival.

The following morning, around 8.15am, several hundred people had gathered outside the cathedral to watch as the icon set off on the first stage of her journey, to the church at Monte. Our Lady of Fatima was now encased in a glass carriage (the sort we euphemistically refer to as a 'Popemobile') for her journey up into the mountains. As the vehicle moved off, a polite burst of spontaneous applause was given, the sort which might be given to any visiting dignitary.

*

Away from Funchal, In the towns and villages of the island, association with the church, processions and religious observance is still more keenly practised. Here, I am told, young people are more likely to be found actively involved in the life of the parish. These rural parishes often hold their own unique processional events.

> *In the course of the year each important parish has its own procession. That of our parish, St. Martinho, takes place on Palm Sunday, and traverses the main roads of the district ... A feature of this as of some other processions is a band of female penitents who, closely veiled in black and bare-footed, walk the stony paths in much discomfort. The cortège reaches the steep road at the back of our house at nightfall, the candles and lanterns are lighted, and to the music of a monotonous dirge the long line of lights slowly ascends the hill, affording a very impressive spectacle.*

One of the oldest examples of this sort of parochial procession, dating back to the seventeenth century, is the feast in honour of Our Lady of Bom Despacho, in Campanario. It's held each year in September and begins uniquely with an early morning hike into the mountains, to the neighbouring parish of Quinta Grande. There, thousands of wild pink lilies (familiarly known as Belladonna) are picked, which are then processed, a sea of pink petals, the ten kilometres back to the small chapel at Campanario. Here the scented lilies decorate the inside and outside of the church, with Mass and a further procession held on the following Sunday.

The Festa da Senhora do Monte is another traditional annual festival with a procession, which attracts several thousand tourists who come to join in the celebration. Sadly, the Festival came to the world's attention in 2017 when a tree fell on participants, killing twelve people.

Not all events will have the same international appeal. During a visit to the little fishing village of Caniçal, we happened to arrive just in time to see a procession about to begin, in celebration of the Feast of St Sabastian. This usually occurs around the third week of January.

Having encountered difficulty parking owing to the volume of traffic in the narrow streets, we emerged from the car to the accompaniment of church choral music, broadcast on a very efficient loudspeaker system. As we walked towards the waterfront, the procession was beginning to form outside the church. All was solemn and silent as the congregation lined up behind the clergy and choir. It then began, at a slow walking pace, making its way through the winding streets of Caniçal.

Despite the solemn nature of the occasion, you couldn't escape the feeling that one huge street party was just about to take place, put temporarily on hold, while observance of the religious elements of the day was satisfied. Not far from where the procession had just moved off, poncha stalls were already being prepared to offer the required 'units' of alcohol to get any party aglow. Nearby, the open-air butcher's counters had cuts of prime beef, hung from hooks, on makeshift rails.

As the procession came to an end, participants were able to take refreshment with a poncha or beer. Once suitably refreshed, they moved on to sample the steak, which they cooked for themselves over one of the many glowing half-oil-drum barbecues. This was a communal picnic on a grand scale, one huge street party, all invited, and very well organised.

To me, it seemed that the old religious order and a more modern secular culture had somehow found common ground. However, I was to discover that the idea of God and Mammon sitting comfortably together was not a new concept at all, and was one which would have been quite familiar to C. T.-S.

> These processions, and the festas of their parochial churches, are almost the only public amusements of the populace. They never lose their attraction. On every such occasion thousands of country-folk tramp many miles to the scene

– romeiros (literally "pilgrims to Rome") they call themselves. And the Church in no way frowns on a combination of innocent amusement with religious exercise. The ordinary adjuncts of a fair are present. Cheapjacks ply their trade, lottery-mongers conduct raffles for dolls and other toys, vendors of fruit and sweetmeats line the walls. The holy-day and the holiday are still one.

Caniçal is also the location for the Festa da Nossa Senhora da Piedade, usually held in September, and dedicated to the fishermen. Here the action takes place by sea, with boats processing between Caniçal to the chapel at Quinta do Lorde.

These are just a very few of the processions a visitor may encounter throughout the year.

*

Given the significance of the religious procession in Madeiran culture, it's not too surprising to discover that there is also something of a secular culture for processing, very similar in nature to that of many Mediterranean countries. With the benefit of a mild, temperate climate, people are more likely to promenade (which is itself a form of procession) in small family groups. This is most apparent throughout the Christmas season, when everyone enjoys an evening stroll to see the coloured lights and the ornamental seasonal displays.

Carnival offers a similar opportunity. Madeiran 'Carnaval' has long been associated with the season of Lent, celebrated here since earliest times going back to the island's golden sugar era. The centrepiece of the week-long festivities is now the Saturday parade with the traditional procession of decorated floats, dancers and musicians. This addition to 'Carnaval' is much more recent. It began not long after the island became an autonomous region and is now one of the highlights of the tourist calendar.

The week is given over to lively street music and entertainments, not just in Funchal. The Compadres Parade in Santana, which starts the Carnival week, has already been mentioned. For the main parade in Funchal, tiered stadium-like seating lines sections of the Avenida do Mar. As usual, most of the island seems to turn out for the event, creating an atmosphere of significance for the occasion. The parade begins around 8 p.m. and lasts for over two hours. As a spectacle of colour, energy and choreography, it's a spectacular floor show and worthy of its springtime position in the tourist calendar.

Aside from the number of participants, the scale of costuming and the set-building of floats is a massive undertaking for the various associations who collaborate to stage the event. It is easy to imagine an entire industry of designers, costume makers and choreographers hard at work for a large part of the year in preparation. The accompanying music shows deep Latin roots with the costumes robustly constructed to cope with the rigours of the dancing. During an impromptu after-parade event, we watched as the dancers clambered into their costumes. They resembled something akin to a lightweight harness, with arms and legs contorted, to don the required metal frames of feathered wings, full skirts and elaborate headdresses. They looked neither easy nor especially comfortable to wear, with occasional minor repairs necessary en route.

*

A Madeiran Sunday still has much of a 'day of rest' feel to it, which in Britain is now a thing of the past. Most non-tourist shops on the island close, although the larger supermarkets, especially in Funchal, have adopted an 'open most hours' policy, commonplace elsewhere. The feel of the city lies somewhere between the French, who close everything, and the UK, which regards Sunday as just another trading day. Unlike France, however, the frequency of bank holidays is very much more in line with the UK, with additional public holidays occurring on 10 June (Portugal Day), 1 July (Madeira Day) and 1 December (Independence Day).

The weather in Funchal encourages an outdoor lifestyle and the parks and promenades on Sundays are convenient meeting places for the elderly and young alike, with the latter taking the free time to practise the ancient art of courtship. In his book, C. T.-S ended his review of 'April – Holy-days and Holidays' with an endearing description of the courtship rituals of the early twentieth century.

> *Portuguese women ... possess a "sweete attractive kinde of grace". For in the spring the young man's fancy lightly turns to thoughts of standing in the street beneath the window of his lady-love. The musical serenade has gone out of fashion, which is a pity; and the lover sometimes cuts, it must be*

owned, a rather ridiculous figure kicking his heels in front of closed shutters, through which the lady, unseen herself, is probably inspecting him. As the shades of evening descend the fair often becomes more kind; the shutters are thrown back and half a female form protrudes from the window. The lover stands immediately below with his head turned upwards at what must be a very uncomfortable angle, and courtship proceeds. This sort of thing may go on for an indefinite period. In the case of a great, and very coy, heiress, it is said to have lasted five hours a day for five years ... The man in the street commonly has an air of being rather bored; but this may be "manners" and a mask to conceal the fierce tumult of his southern blood. When the affair has been officially brought to the notice of the lady's parents by some friend of the gentleman's family, and terms have been satisfactorily arranged, the lover is at length admitted to the house, an engagement is ratified, and marriage follows at no distant date. But here as elsewhere, following the American and English mode, the manners and customs of the jeune fille are becoming more free and easy, and probably before long the fashion of craning necks at windows will be a thing of the past.

There is just a slight hint of Jane Austen about all this, with the fashion of courtship clearly showing signs of the need for modernisation. As one might expect, in the city today, the sight of a young man *"kicking his heels in front of closed shutters"*, in the hope of winning over a lady love, is most definitely consigned to the history books.

My morning walk along the Avenida do Mar gives me a chance to observe current trends at first hand. Young couples are invariably found in various forms of embrace, as they wait together, killing time before taking the bus to school or making their separate ways to work. The space of the great outdoors, even in what they call winter, gives them a distinct advantage over those from northern Europe. No more separated by shutters, they can bill and coo, seemingly oblivious to anything around them.

The modern accompaniment of the 'smart' phone is, of course, ever-present. Clutched protectively, one feels it's almost like a modern-day rosary. It's a distraction which is put to good use when the attention being shown becomes a little more than wished for. To have a partner more interested in the phone than their companion seems the perfect ploy to dampen anyone's ardour. In courtship, as with most other things, all is now so very much twenty-first century, with *"the ladies"*, thankfully, no longer leading the *"very secluded lives"* of the past.

April. Mountains and Islands.

In the chapter 'January – Town and Country Delights', C. T.-S. took us on an afternoon's picnic to Ribeiro Frio. With the days lengthening and more settled weather, he is taking the Mount Railway again (to follow, we must now take the cable car, taxi or bus), up into the cooler air, to Monte, from where

> *you may take a hundred walks, to little peaks and minor valleys ... If you are more ambitious, you may ascend from the Mount by what I have already described as the main road to the north side. When you emerge from the pine-woods on to the moorland you will see the track ahead of you for miles, skirting ridge after ridge, and ever ascending. Not long since it was a mere horse-path, but it is gradually being paved, and is attaining to the dignity of a road. To the contemplative mind it will suggest something of the past history of the island. Doubtless the early settlers would not be long before they strove to cross the mountains, and it is not improbable that this was the route they would take, and that today we are treading in their footsteps.*

On this occasion, his destination was the Nun's Valley, as regular a stop-off on island tours today as it has been for many years.

> *The best known and perhaps the oftenest attempted excursion from Funchal is to the Grand Curral, called by the Portuguese Curral das Freiras, "the Nuns' Fold", from the Convent of Santa Clara having formerly possessed considerable property in it. It is a deep valley, of more or less circular shape, almost in the centre of the island, and bounded on its northern curve by the highest peaks. At its lower end it contracts to a gorge too narrow to admit of a road. It is therefore necessary to ascend the enclosing hills on one side or the other, east or west, to obtain a view of the valley. Neither excursion conducts the traveller to any great height, the former to an altitude of about 3300 feet, the latter to about 4400 feet. The eastern side being nearer to Funchal is more often visited. It is perhaps the pleasanter ride, but the western side affords the finer view. From either point one looks down into the great basin, with its strip of cultivation and its little church standing on its floor 2000 feet above the sea; the encircling mountains scarred with fissures from base to summit, and culminating on all sides in towers and pinnacles of rock.*

The first views of the Nun's Valley are usually found from an elevated vantage point on the south-eastern side. On a clear day, it's too easy to forget that the village far below is inhabited. It seems to resemble a Lilliputian model, almost a child's plaything, with visitors about to take on the role of Jonathan Swift's mythical character, Gulliver.

But such thoughts are quickly dispelled by the insignificance one feels when gazing up from the village itself. Sheer walls seem to encase the valley. It's like being marooned in some mighty vat or cauldron. Access is via a single road, leading to the valley floor, where no further excursion is possible. There's no alternative other than to retrace one's steps. Only the river successfully makes a meandering escape via an alternative route, to emerge at a point east of Camara de Lobos, where it meets the sea.

The journey up and down into this 'pudding basin' of a valley is remarkable. It's possible to glimpse short sections of the original old road clinging to the rock face as if adhered by some mystical force. A mountaineer traversing a difficult crevasse would undoubtedly look for greater security than these mere ledges would once have offered. They serve only as a reminder of the days of foot or horse-drawn transport.

It is not altogether impossible to believe that, in previous generations, there were some living in the Grand Curral who had never set eyes on the sea, despite its relative proximity. Before the advent of the motor engine (and a serviceable road), a more isolated spot one couldn't imagine. Great exertion would have been necessary to escape its seclusion by foot. Were the valley to be found, say, in the highlands of Scotland, one could imagine lengthy periods of the year when it would be cut off, all access impossible. Little wonder the nuns, who once lived here, and after whom the valley is affectionately known, felt that this wall-like barrier gave adequate protection against the marauding pirates who frequented the coastal regions.

Once back out of the valley, it's possible to trace the perimeter rim by road, eventually arriving at Pico do Arieiro. There are several stop-off points along this road. Frequently, you may find yourself above the clouds, surrounded by some very surreal images as peaks protrude above a ghostly void. This was certainly an experience familiar to C. T.-S.

> *It frequently happens that while a thin belt of clouds hangs round the mountains and over the sea at an elevation of three or four thousand feet, the peaks themselves stand clear above it … And then perchance the spectator may behold a wonderful sight; gazing out to sea, as far as the eye can reach, he may look down upon the sunlit upper surface of the cloud-belt, an ocean of fleecy brilliance. Such a glorious spectacle is no mean compensation for the loss of a view of the lower hills and the coast.*

Such a scene is one which any airline passenger, or at least those with window seats, can readily appreciate, as the aircraft rises above the canopy of cloud. This is not to detract from the magnificence of the views from Pico Arieiro without a base of cloud, but the vastness of a billowy, diaphanous wasteland puts the watcher in mind of the loneliness of some vast frozen continent. This image of infinite, inhospitable isolation is so much easier to appreciate from a safe vantage point and without the freezing conditions accompanying reality.

*

The seas around Madeira are equally expansive, broken up by a group of islands to the south-east. The Madeiran island archipelago comprises two inhabited islands, Madeira and Porto Santo, the nearby uninhabited Desertas Islands, and then, about 280 kilometres away, also to the south-east, the Savage Islands.

> *Midway between Madeira and the Canaries lies a small group of three uninhabited Islands, the Savages, to which a different sort of interest attaches. In 1820 a dying sailor made a confession that Captain Kidd, the celebrated pirate, had buried a great quantity of treasure there. Various attempts have been made to discover it, without success; and if the dying sailor was not playing a practical joke on the world he was leaving, it still remains to tempt the adventurous.*

The Savage Islands were probably too far away to be seriously within C. T.-S.'s contemplation of making a visit. These islands are now a protected nature reserve and a UNESCO World Heritage Site. As a result, other than to the scientists working there, they are only accessible with permission. Any treasure hunters today will be left forever disappointed!

The Desertas Islands, on the other hand, lie a mere 15 miles (18 km) south-east of Madeira. Anyone walking the waterfront of Funchal on a clear day cannot fail to find their eyes being automatically drawn to these sizeable landmasses. For those with time, there's also the opportunity to plan a visit.

> *The rise of the full moon over the Desertas, with a garden for foreground, and her broad belt of silvery light upon the sea beyond, is indeed a glorious spectacle, perhaps hardly to be matched elsewhere.*

> *The uninhabited islands ... which are such a prominent object in the view from Funchal and the hills above it ... contain a race of wild goats, descendants, it is said, of domestic goats placed on them by Columbus ... These goats are fine big fellows, carrying grand heads, and often nearly black in colour. The islands are private property and the shooting is preserved, a fairly easy matter considering the difficulty of access to them. It is a journey of some three hours in a steam-launch from Funchal to the usual landing place, and if there is much surf, landing there is by no means a certainty at the end of it, and it may be necessary to scramble ashore at the foot of some inhospitable cliff, and make one's way up as best one can. The islands have very little vegetation and less fresh water, but goats are not very particular. The scenery has a very weird unfinished appearance, suggesting a picture of the world after the subsidence of the Deluge. The usual method of shooting is to take one's stand on the narrow plateau at the top of the island, almost 1100 feet above the sea-level, and to shoot down at the goats which are driven along the rocks almost perpendicularly below, not a very easy kind of shooting for those unaccustomed to it.*

> *The caves of the larger island are inhabited by a species of seal (Monachus albiventer), the only mammal, with the exception of two species of bats, indigenous to the Madeiras.*

Visiting the Desertas today, one must also have permission, as it is a protected nature reserve, with only a small area available for those keen to go ashore. Recently, however, an option for a one-night stay has also become possible and is likely to be very popular with marine bird enthusiasts. These islands are about two to three hours' sailing time from Funchal, a passage I was able to make in a 23-metre, wooden-hulled, two-mast gullet, of 99 tons. The south-eastern stretch of water can be fickle at times, and in winter months, the Porto Santo ferry, even with its capacity for 1100 passengers and 145 vehicles, may be confined to port, or forced to return, rather than complete the short passage.

We sailed along the coast east of Funchal until we were about level with Caniço, before heading south-south-east into more open waters. In the distance to the east, we could soon make out the grainy outline of Porto Santo. We were sailing into light winds and a slight swell, which repeatedly pushed the boat's nose one way then the other. It was like a boxer toying with an inferior sparring partner, providing us with a gentle rocking motion.

A flock of gulls, some floating, others flying a metre or so above the sea, appeared from nowhere. At first, it looked as if they had discovered a shoal of fish and that we were about to be entertained by a feeding frenzy, but as none appeared to dive, that idea was quickly dispelled. Instead, they continued to keep pace with us, always maintaining a safe distance. It was almost as if they were checking us out, like an advance guard, observing our intentions. Then, their task seemingly completed, they disappeared almost as quickly.

It was in searching to discover where they had flown that I happened to look back, for the first time, towards the Bay of Funchal. We were at about the point where, I would imagine, C. T.-S., coming to the end of his three-day passage from Southampton, would have had his first proper sighting of his destination. Today, a horizontal line of cloud, a little above Monte, hung like a mantelpiece, with the highest peaks protruding above it. Even on a clear day, these are not visible to anyone on the Funchal waterfront.

From ten to fifteen miles out at sea, Madeira's full magnificence is more dramatically put on show, and is one of the most impressive views of the island. To glimpse that familiar silhouette once more would have made the passage worthwhile, no matter how rigorous their crossing of the Bay of Biscay might have been. To share in that view, from the main southern sea access route, served to conjure up all the excitement that C. T.-S. must have experienced on so many occasions. It is only from sea level, on a clear day, that one can fully appreciate how imposing is Funchal's hillside and the dominating range of mountains which forms its backdrop.

This moment was suddenly broken by the shouts of the crew. Their eyes were fixed, and they were pointing to the west. The engines were slowed, and the wheel swung the bow to starboard. A pod of shimmering silver dolphins was showing off, slipping effortlessly in and out of the glistening sea just ahead of us. For the next fifteen minutes or so, these would-be 'pilots' navigated our course in the direction of the Desertas, and we followed as if under escort.

The Desertas Islands are often only a rudimentary outline on the horizon from Funchal, frequently hidden from view by haze. Now, only a few miles off, they began to show individual characteristics. There are three islands, each markedly different from the other. All three would, at some time, have joined the mainland in one long chain, stretching out beyond Ponta de São Lourenço's far south-eastern 'fingertip'.

Chão Island has sheer cliffs like walls all around and a top which, from sea level, appears as flat as any billiard table. It was probably just an optical illusion, as we didn't get close enough to see the baize of the cloth. Deserta Grande has many similarities with Madeira, but unlike the mainland, it is almost totally barren. The exposed surfaces show more obvious signs of the volcanic eruptions which took place millions of years ago. As we travelled almost the length of its western coastline, it reminded me of an old-fashioned milk pudding, cooked in a bowl that was too small. The result was an overflow, now a burnt crust, baked hard on the bowl's outer surface. Last of all, there is Bugio Island, with many fine needle-sharp peaks and pinnacles.

It is towards the southern tip, where Grande and Bugio come closest, that access for visitors is totally prohibited. Here the monk seals (Monachus monachus) and Desertas petrels have their breeding grounds and they enjoy the habitat undisturbed.

> *A year or two ago [a seal] was offered for sale in Funchal. It was purchased and placed in a pond in a garden some four hundred feet above the sea. It speedily became very tame, and would take its food from the hands of the young ladies of the house. But it sighed (if seals sigh) for the freedom of its native Atlantic, and the comfortable cave in the Desertas wherein to repose, perhaps for the society of its kind ... its plea for liberty was not in vain; and shortly after ... [it was returned] to the sea in the neighbourhood of the Desertas, where we may hope it found its mate still faithful to its memory, and lives happy ever after.*

Driven almost to extinction in the 1980s, the protection afforded by Madeira has meant that these seals do indeed survive, with sightings not only along the shores of the Desertas but also, once more, along the island's southern coastal regions.

We moored for a few hours in the Doca, a man-made sound, with a sheltered cove leading onto a flat level shelf, beneath another sheer cliff face. The Reserve Rangers have their accommodation built here. I don't know why, but as I looked at this single-storey building, my mind went back to the pictures of Shackleton and Scott's accommodation on the Ross Island shelf in Antarctica. Dwarfed by the surrounding landscape, they were almost inconsequential in a hostile, barren environment. Isolated and alone, working in small groups, two weeks on and two weeks off, I imagine the Madeiran Rangers find the arrival of occasional summer tourists a very welcome relief to the monotony of the winter months.

We took the opportunity to 'step ashore'. This meant slipping inelegantly over the side of an inflatable tender, barefoot and with shoes tied securely around our necks, to paddle ashore like novice explorers.

We were to discover, despite what C. T.-S. had written about shooting parties preying on the goats for sport, the visitors of the early 1900s had surprisingly not brought about the demise of the goat population. They flourish on the hilltops, "eating everything in sight", which perhaps explains the barren appearance of Grande. It seems incredible to think that while man couldn't live on the island due to a lack of available drinking water, these goats have found the landscape quite conducive; nevertheless, they must be thankful now the guns are silent. Today all is peace and quiet, and the goats share this mountainous terrain with a type of tarantula spider.

A short wander along a nature trail offered few encounters with any of the wildlife, but provided good information about the island's habitat. Before long, it was time to wade back to the inflatable tender. Getting off was considerably easier than clambering 'on'. I watched as several undignified contortions were assumed by those higher up the queue. By the time it came to my turn, I had already decided that there was no right or wrong way, trusting to making it aboard with nothing more serious than a damp hind-quarter.

The cruise back to Funchal was without interruption. The dolphins had provided their one performance for the day and were not inclined to offer any encores. As for the other sea mammals found in these waters, they merely sent their apologies. It did mean we had the chance to share once again the full experience of the approach to Funchal from the sea.

It took a little over two hours to travel back. At first, Funchal was barely discernible through a haze, caused as much by distance as weather. From the airport to the Bay of Funchal, it seemed that some form of habitation now lined the entire coastal regions.

Funchal advanced at a steady pace as we made our leisurely and sedate progress, with plenty of time to savour the moments. There are few distractions. The sea, when flat calm, gives little to hold the attention. You can watch, mesmerised for hours, as an angry sea pounds against rocks, but there's only so much amusement to be found in a becalmed ocean. Sails were unfurled and hoisted; I'm sure only to enhance our experience. It was the motor which provided our greatest means of momentum.

From a distance, the city is just a blend of darkness and light; dark the hills and trees; light the houses. Buildings lack individuality, just a patchwork of different blocks of white, pink, grey and black. At, I would imagine, about five miles out, however, the buildings start to become a little more distinguishable.

The two church spires (Santo Antonio and São Martinho) dominate Funchal's western horizon, as if intentionally placed in a line to make perfect aids to navigation. The closer one gets, the more of the city's detail is revealed, but even then, the perspective is so very flat. You appreciate nothing of the ridges and ravines, many of which hide vast swathes of buildings in their folds. At any one time, a sizeable proportion of Funchal is hidden from view, giving the impression of a slightly less crowded hillside than is the case.

The persistent clouds can't resist imposing themselves, through which the setting sun, drenching individual pockets of the hillside, turns them into the richest of molten-liquid golden glows. Perhaps it was a sight such as this that C. T.-S. had in mind when he quoted the lines of Oliver Goldsmith:

As some tall cliff that lifts its awful form,
Swells from the vale, and midway leaves the storm,
Though round its breast the rolling clouds are spread,
Eternal sunshine settles on its head.

Arrival within port limits takes one slightly by surprise. Perhaps it is in becoming accustomed to the deceptive pace of progress, where everything appears to be conducted in slow motion, that you suddenly appreciate the point of disembarkation or anchorage is nearer than anticipated, causing reality to descend in quick time, and a hasty gathering together of personal belongings.

Back on dry land, there's the need to remind oneself that the quay has not taken on a gentle rolling motion, it's just that the brain has failed to adjust to reality as quickly as everything else, all of which brings another adventure, also experienced by C. T.-S., to a suitable end.

April. The Garden in its Glory.

Is there one month, over any other, which shows Madeira's gardens at the height of their perfection? Each month described by C. T.-S. has its attractions, as I hope has been revealed in these pages. Nevertheless, seeing the beauty and splendour of the flowers at their dazzling best is, for many, one of the reasons for coming in the first place.

For C. T.-S., April was a month when summer blooms were more likely to be found at their freshest and in profusion. He gave us the full tour of his own garden in April, describing fragrances and vibrant, delicate-petalled beauties, almost too perfect for us to imagine.

> *The Madeira garden in April exhibits at once a high midsummer pomp, and the exuberant if delicate freshness of spring. Most of the standard garden flowers, however manfully they have striven to shed glory on the winter months, are greeting April with a redoubled show of vigour. The garden beds are a mass of brilliant colour – salvias, petunias, stocks, snapdragons, geraniums, pelargoniums, and a hundred others are in full bloom ...*

> *Lilies of many kinds are coming up, though May is perhaps the month of their pre-eminence. But a beautiful speckled amaryllis, of which we imported a few bulbs some years ago, has multiplied itself a hundred-fold, and has chosen April as its flowering season.*

> *Roses we have had always with us, but since December not in such a glorious profusion as now. An arch clothed with Maréchal Niel, hanging its delicate blooms in hundreds is a very beautiful sight. William Allen Richardson has risen from a well-earned repose to cover a long pergola with buds of a richer and deeper hue. The single white levigata is sprinkling our fences with discs of snow-white purity; Reine Marie Henriette queens it among her rivals; in velvety richness Bardou Job asserts an unquestioned pre-eminence.*

> *Three very beautiful species of Bignonia are now flowering ... The soft yellow Tweediana is everywhere, a blaze of colour at many a street-corner. If less insistent in colour than the glorious orange venusta, the queen of*

December and January, it may yet in its great refinement be more pleasing to many eyes. Purpurea, a species with mauve flowers of exquisite refinement, offers a pleasant contrast.

His descriptions of the blossoming of summer were not confined to the cultivated gardens. At this time of year, colour also filled busy streets, alleys and quiet corners. Urbanisation has deprived us of a great deal of what C. T.-S. would have seen growing quite naturally, but it is nevertheless worth immersing oneself in the verbal scenes he paints, to picture the walls, terraces and verandas, all brought to life in a mass of colour.

At this season nothing is more supremely lovely than the Wistaria, now in full pride of its vernal freshness, and endowed with a notable grace and distinction which are all its own. Its delicate shading and its variations of hue in different lights make it the despair of almost all the many artists whose efforts to depict it we watch with interest. It has been freely planted of recent years, and may now be seen everywhere, with a serene impartiality hanging over dull walls in mean streets, and clambering over tall magnolia trees in stately gardens. Perhaps it is most charming when covering a long railing on a terrace. In such a situation you may look down upon, or up to, its dense masses of bloom, as the fancy takes you.

I can't help feeling that, for C. T.-S., his most treasured time of day would have been early evening. Surrounded by these fragrant blossoms; assessing the day's achievements and making plans for the next; perhaps admiring the view out to sea towards the Desertas Islands, on which a full moon had furnished its *"belt of silvery light"*. It's a view quite capable of captivation, to be savoured for as long as possible, as twilight descends into nightfall.

And the splendid sky of the northern hemisphere, "the mild assemblage of the starry heavens", is to be seen at its best in this clear air ... Moon or no moon, the hours

"From evensong to daytime
When April melts in Maytime,"
[A. C. Swinburne]

are fairer than the day, however fair. And the pleasant hour of nightfall lacks in this equitable climate that dangerous chill which is common in

> *Mediterranean and African countries. The twilight is, of course, less prolonged than in northern lands, but the night comes with less haste than in the tropics; and even if clouds have obscured the mountain-tops during the day, they generally disperse at sunset, and the line of peaks stands hard and clear against the sky ...*
>
> *Of white blossoms none surpass in delicacy and grace the hanging bells of the Datura. Throughout the winter they have appeared once a month to greet the full moon, but for the April moon they have reserved their most liberal profusion. And now they give forth their most pungent odours – odours almost overpowering at nightfall, when all the garden scents are strongest. This habit of flowering at the full moon appears to be not merely legendary, but fact; and the Datura would seem to be gifted with a feminine capacity for knowing what becomes her, for she never shows her beauties to greater advantage than by moonlight.*

It's difficult to read this passage without a slight feeling of drowsiness descending. So, let's quickly dispel any heavy-eyed soporific tendencies. April was the final month of his stay on the island, and with so much more to be seen and done, sleep should be the last thing on anyone's mind.

*

Whether April be the best month, for the present we will allow that to remain a subjective opinion; nevertheless, it is an ideal time to visit some of the quinta gardens, to see them at the start of their elegant best and to appreciate their individual, subtle variations.

> *The gardens of Funchal and its neighbourhood are not only ... all different, they are, in fact, of quite surprisingly various character. Some are remarkable especially for their collections of trees and shrubs from many countries and many climes; others for the dignity imparted by the growth of a century; others again for the success with which flowering plants are cultivated.*

Many of today's quintas were familiar to C. T.-S. and a very small number are described in this chapter. The gardens at Quinta Jardins do Lago (formerly known as the Quinta d'Achada) were first set out in the eighteenth century. At one time, this was the residence of the Commander of the British forces during the Napoleonic Wars. Today, it is a luxury hotel which maintains two-and-a-half acres of lush botanical garden.

> *The Quinta d'Achada, "the level" is described by its name. It is unique among Madeira gardens in occupying a nearly level tract on the top of a ridge between two ravines. With its fine and spacious old house, its magnificent groups of such shrubs as Strelitzia augusta, here of a size and perfection not to be met with elsewhere, its pleasant walks, its wealth of water, and the view from its terrace over the eastern half of the city and of the hills above, it may perhaps strike the visitor as the most desirable of all the Quintas of Funchal.*

It remains as impressive today, and a convenient short taxi ride from central Funchal. As a tranquil spot for afternoon tea, or a holiday, it would tick all of the boxes. Invariably, as with most city quintas, the location would have been uppermost in selecting the site. Quinta Jardins do Lago has unobstructed views of the bay. It is an unhurried oasis, set among lush green foliage, complete with a giant Galapagos tortoise, appropriate in a place where even time can afford to wait awhile.

The Strelitzia is still a feature of this Quinta's garden. The Strelitzia augusta or nicolai (the Gigante White Bird of Paradise) is spectacular: a tree-sized strelitzia, of similar proportion to a mature banana. It's almost disproportionately sized white flower-head is in marked contrast to the rather petite common Strelitzia reginae, which we are more accustomed to find in floral displays. The Gigante is unmistakably a member of the strelitzia family, but without any features which might suggest a 'bird of paradise'. In the case of the Gigante, it would undoubtedly be a winged creature from the Jurassic Age, were it ever to take flight.

Walking the garden, with its meandering miniature levada and water features, it is difficult to contemplate a time when open fields and farms would once have surrounded it. Swish apartments sit opposite the hotel entrance, where once sugar and grapes would have flourished.

Quinta Vigia, another of those mentioned by C. T.-S., has the advantage over many others in being the closest to the port and central Funchal. Previously known as the Quinta Angustias, the pink watchtower is a distinctive landmark perched atop the cliff, above the

CR7 museum and hotel. For day tourists, a clifftop glance in the direction of the tower is possibly the nearest most will come to visiting one of the island's quintas.

Quinta Vigia's small gardens are manicured and maintained with the sort of tender care one might expect of a Presidential Residence. Perhaps understandably, it does not go out of its way to let you know that the public are welcome. That may be just as well. If coachloads were to begin arriving, not only would the gardens quickly become swamped, but you might imagine security would look to impose some sort of restriction on numbers.

As things stand at present, having paid the small entrance fee, one can wander around the little shaded pebbled paths, bordered by flower beds. Delicate sweet peas were being thinned out, but not the straggly variety we tend to encourage to climb around bamboo canes in the style of an English cottage garden. Here they are more bushlike, rising no more than twelve inches from the soil. To carpet rather than climb is the preferred way here of showing off these most delicate of flowers.

It is a remarkably peaceful place, especially given the proximity of the busy Avenida do Infante. Somehow, it manages to banish most of the intrusive bustle of city life going on a few metres away. Commercial buses thunder their laborious diesel-fed way up and down the Avenida, and perspiring pedestrians climb the steep ascent on their way back to their respective hotels after a day's sightseeing. The trees perform a useful job in screening out some of this urban noise, helped by the gardens falling gradually away toward the sea, so that most of the noise simply passes overhead.

The water features play a small part too. The sound of running water has a magical quality. It can lower temperatures and muffle out unwanted background noise, and in this case they enhance the garden's private seclusion. At the southern corner, the gardens end abruptly with a boundary wall, below which a sheer cliff falls away to the port area. Throughout much of the winter, this escarpment's edge has had a mantle of magenta coloured bougainvillea draped over its wide shoulders. It's not surprising C. T.-S. should have written of the place,

> *... nothing can impair the charm of its unique position on a cliff above the port.*

It is interesting to note that many of the quintas about which C. T.-S. wrote have either fallen into decline, reverted to private residences or been adapted for other purposes. It is part of the history of the Madeiran quinta that fortunes rise and fall and sometimes rise and then fall again. In some cases, this has required a total rebuild'; in others, renovation. This was certainly the case with Quinta Vigia.

> *The Quinta Vigia, possessing in former days perhaps the most admired and famous of Madeira gardens, has fallen from its high estate. It was put for some years to the base use of a casino ... and since left more or less derelict, it has lost much of the beauty which it once enjoyed.*

The same could be said of the Quinta, now the Quintinha (somewhat smaller than a quinta) São João, another of those described by C. T.-S. and, again, a short taxi ride from central Funchal.

> *The Quinta S. Joao is remarkable for the quiet dignity of the approach from the entrance gate to the house – a perfectly level and straight road bordered by palms and tropical trees, a delicious line of restful greenery.*

Much of the *"quiet dignity"* these days has been sadly lost, certainly during weekdays, as a busy main road hugs the south-western perimeter wall. The *"sumptuous avenue of trees that leads to the main entrance of the quinta, which was one of the most notable in the city"* referred to in the book *Origins of Tourism in Madeira*, sadly has been lost.

Today a five-star classical-style spa hotel sits alongside the Quintinha, complete with all the cherished furnishings one might expect from a close association with such a lovely old manorial home. The Quintinha itself is a private residence.

At various times, the Quintinha São João went into decline, only for new owners to revive its fortunes. During one such period of decline, permission was given to build a more modern hotel close to its eastern boundary. The current hotel (The Four Views) is not the first to occupy the space, but it deprives the Quintinha of its spectacular views of Funchal Bay.

The Quintinha's hotel and spa must have eaten into a large proportion of the gardens. An original tiled entrance is now almost lost along the south garden perimeter wall and is no longer in use. With a little imagination, one can appreciate what the approach to the Quintinha might have been like. To compensate for what has been lost, however, the Quintinha's hotel provides an especially homely, cosy afternoon tea!

In mentioning just a few of the quintas, it is hoped that the appetite will be well whetted, and that visitors will wish to venture out and discover more for themselves. As mentioned earlier, there are many to choose from, and by no means all are in Funchal. A holiday spent doing nothing other than visiting the quintas and their gardens could occupy as much time as anyone might wish to spare. Comparing grounds and gardens could make this more enjoyable and make for a very different but delightful short vacation. A visit to any Tourist Information Office will provide enough details of quintas worth visiting.

For those taking up the suggestion, C. T.-S. provides some useful general insights into the characteristics of the formal quinta garden. These are certainly reflections worth packing away in one's mental rucksack for future reference.

> *These gardens are but a tithe of those which surround the town [Funchal] on all sides, gardens greater and less, gardens English and Portuguese, gardens of varying purpose and differing ideals. But the traveller who is fortunate enough to see them will carry away an impression of horticultural variety and beauty which is probably unique. And of each it may be emphatically said that it is the right thing in the right place. Each is appropriate to the position it occupies, to the house of which it is the pleasure ground; there is no straining after unnatural effect; no "laying-out" by a landscape gardener with theories to illustrate.*

> *With the ancient contest between the "formalist" and the "naturalist" we have little concern. The gardens are one and all of necessity formal; the retaining wall insures that ... "Naturalization" is quite out of place where the soil has to be held in terraces. Where it is appropriate, as on the rocky cliffs of ravines ... it may be eminently successful. In such situations, aloes, and cactus, and "Pride of Madeira", and valerian, and heliotrope will clothe the rocks with wild luxuriance, and fight a desperate struggle for the mastery.*

> *The pergola, or corridor, is here in its natural home. It was primarily built in the unsophisticated days for one of two purposes, often combined, either to*

shade a path from the hot summer sun, or to afford a support for vines. It was then constructed of square stone pillars with an open roof of chestnut wood. It has unfortunately been found cheaper, and in native opinion neater, to substitute iron rods for the stone columns ... In Madeira, where the chief glory of our gardens is their wealth of brilliant-flowered climbers, and shade from the sub-tropical sun is a necessity, there is no question as to their appropriateness ...

The arrangement of garden paths is a somewhat elaborate and expensive business ... The orthodox plan is to pave the paths with small flattish cobble-stones which are rammed into the earth in close proximity, so as to form a solid pavement. According to ancient custom, patterns are formed of lines and circles, often of lighter coloured stones. The effect is pleasing, and a good solid path is the result ...

It may be that a reliance on regularity and symmetry in decoration is a note of ... an unimaginative nature. Certainly to arrange things in pairs, lines or rows, or circles calls for less intellectual effort than arranging them unsymmetrically ... Perhaps we may conclude that it has its due place, but that it is unsuitable to the arrangement of plants in a garden.

And with that passing jibe, April – and his time on the island – was coming to an end. I am sure he could have managed to stay longer, but to delay departure would have meant missing all that a springtime in England had to offer.

Despite the frequent chill of an English spring day, what could tempt him to let such a dramatic reawakening slip by unobserved? That is not to underestimate the sadness he must have felt as the moment of departure beckoned. He knew what he was leaving behind, and after five months, we can assume a little more than Madeiran soil would have slipped under his fingernails. There is one occasion in the original book where C. T.-S. uses the phrase "*We Madeirans*". This simple phrase probably illustrates better than anything else the degree of attachment he had for the island, a place he regarded as his winter home.

*

So, is April the best month of any to visit this island? Perhaps it is a question that any visitor should really answer for themselves. C. T.-S., does, however, offer us this final clue.

> *Great as is the garden's April glory, we are conscious that we are in the habit of leaving it a little short of perfection. Perfection, we are told, is to be found in May. After that the heats of summer prevail, the garden is dried up, and, until the autumn rains come, no great wealth of garden flowers is to be looked for, however, brilliant the wild flowers of the hills.*

April. Departure.

As the proverb runs, *"There is an end to everything, to good things as well"*, and for C. T.-S. his time on the island had reached its conclusion once more. His visits were always temporary. You detect no intention of making the island a permanent home. Its attractions were the avoidance of North European winters, and the chance to tend a garden all year round. As a bird's migration is triggered by instinct, so too with C. T.-S the imminent arrival of spring back home evoked a natural wish to return.

> *May has its charms elsewhere; even the London parks are "bad to beat". The truth is that the perfect gardener should never leave his garden; every month, every day has its due labour and its due reward.*

And so, the process of preparing to leave would have begun. In this activity, he was not alone. It was an annual ritual shared with hundreds of others, fortunate enough to see out another winter on the island. But he was conscious that it was a lifestyle which he felt was becoming increasingly outdated.

> *Towards the middle of April ... the homeward-bound steamers are full of passengers, and for eight or nine months the land will have rest.*

> *The old days when families came here for the winter and rented quintas and set up house are past. Not only is the servant difficulty acute, but the world is in too great a hurry nowadays for such leisurely experiments. But the number of strangers who pay a visit for a few weeks or a month or two is ever growing. There was a period this winter when the hotel accommodation was strained to the utmost. The hordes of strangers which now swarm in the more attractive parts of the earth's surface, in their due season, suggest a question as to the future of these resorts.*

It's a sad, reflective lament, almost an epitaph to a privileged lifestyle which he felt was not just in decline but would soon disappear altogether. Certainly, by the twenty-first century, we can assume, he would have expected it would have long been consigned to the history books.

But, has this lifestyle disappeared altogether? On Madeira today, one still finds a sizeable community who uproot for a season or part of a season, enjoying the island along with those who have transplanted and taken up permanent residence. Visit Funchal's English Church on any Sunday morning, and you will soon be rubbing shoulders in that calm oasis of Britons at home on foreign soil. The British are by no means alone. Scandinavians relish the chance to escape from their interminable winter darkness, and who can blame them?

Renting a quinta may no longer be the option it once was, although the Quinta de Santa Luzia (and there may be others) sleeps seventeen, and is available to rent for anyone keen to enjoy the full quinta experience. But quintas aside, there is a growing band, especially among the middle-aged retired or semi-retired, who take full advantage of the mild winters that Madeira has to offer, staying for longer than the customary couple of weeks. The hotels have also recognised this emerging market, catering specifically for these month-at-a-time grey-haired 'stay-overs'. Apartments are available to rent for those who enjoy a more independent lifestyle. So, rather than decline, one can almost see a similar market remaining, one accessible to more than just a privileged few.

Perhaps Madeira has always had its special attraction for this age group, and yet the island somehow manages to avoid the 'feel' of some resorts on the south coast of England, which almost seem to exist to accommodate retirees.

> *In our later age we may be drawn rather to reseek the shady side of Pall Mall, the quays by the Arno, or a Madeira garden.*

For anyone thinking about joining Madeira's expatriate community, the idea of renting for a few months, before buying, is surely sound advice. Uprooting from anywhere can come with its pitfalls. Rose-tinted glasses may give a false picture of what to expect. Separation from family (especially grandchildren) and friends; the security issues of leaving either property unoccupied for long periods; coping with a new language in middle age (although in Funchal this has rarely been a problem) can be a challenge that you either relish or take steps to avoid; accepting new customs and procedures; health issues; adapting to a small-island culture, they all represent a change in lifestyle and added pressure that needs to be recognised, when deciding if a permanent move is such a good thing.

Finding all this out before making a costly commitment to purchase will undoubtedly mean saving a great deal of money, not to mention headaches. We have always felt that, unless one plans to stay for more than, say, four months in any year, renting is probably the better solution.

Then there is the uncertainty brought about by Brexit both now and in the future. Restrictions on maximum length of stay; reciprocal health arrangements; state pension regulation, all need to be taken into account.

But then such uncertainties were not too far from the surface even in 1909.

> *The number of more or less leisured people, or people who are able to take a holiday of some weeks at this season, appears to have increased enormously of recent years. And the money they spend abroad even for food alone must represent a serious loss to our purveyors, perhaps inadequately made up by the money strangers spend in the British Isles. When we have a Tariff Reform Government it might appropriately ordain that every British subject temporarily absenting himself from British soil should be required to procure a permit, costing, say a pound sterling for each week. This would make up to the country what it loses by his absence; it would enable the tourist to feel that he was leaving his country for his country's good; it would produce a considerable revenue, and tend at the same time, with that happy double-barrelled effect of protective measures, to protect the English hotel industry ... But it would then be not unreasonable to put an import tax on such introductions ... It is a beautiful idea. Indeed, the possibilities that present themselves as soon as one begins to consider the reform on scientific lines of our antiquated and unimaginative fiscal system are endless.*

Insurance tax, airport tax, they are all in place today, to recoup a little more from those leaving or visiting the country, whether temporarily or permanently.

*

For C. T.-S., the process of packing would have been in full swing. He, of course, would not have been restricted to our narrow baggage allowances. I imagine a significant number of trunks, some the size of a small chest of drawers, would have been carried down from his quinta to a ship's agent's office, either by bearer or hauled by oxen, to await the arrival of the package steamer on which he was booked.

We are given no indication of how much time was spent in packing. To expect him to have brought to the island everything necessary to have occupied his time is unrealistic, but one can assume a sizeable amount of luggage would have accompanied them. Owning a quinta would have meant that many of his possessions would have remained behind, in readiness for the next visit. But, in those days, furniture would have been covered with dust sheets and any valuable ornaments packed away, all of which would have occupied a good deal of time. As we have already seen, for some visitors who had brought furniture and plate with them, some or all of this would have been sold to pay off rent and other debts. A 'car boot' type sale would, therefore, have been arranged at the quinta in advance of departure.

*

Four continuous months is a substantial slice of any year, but perhaps leaving, having already spent a third of the year here, would have been much less of a wrench than, say, at the end of a shorter period. Maybe there was even an element of looking forward to a change of scenery and a return to a more normal life.

> *... the time draws on to the day of our departure. The garden we have tended for four months will be handed over to the unrestrained care of our excellent Carlos for the next eight, and heaven only knows what he will do with it ... But we must take our chance, and in this easy-going land it is quite useless to fuss. We ourselves have other fish to fry, and to catch before we fry them. And until the fogs of November fill us with a longing for the sun, and send us to the steamship office for our passages, Madeira will be but a distant isle of the sea, an isle of pleasant memories and flattering hopes. So may our lives be divided into water-tight compartments.*
>
> *And as the picture of his mistress that the lover carries in his heart may be fairer than the lady herself, so it may be that in the blue haze of the distance the Isle of Beauty will loom more lovely even than she appears to a closer view. We may recall the never-failing perfume of the flowers and forget the occasional odours of the streets; memory may revel in the golden haze of a sunset, and find no place for the mist that chilled us on the hills. In memory which dwells on the agreeable and dismisses the unpleasant, in hope which*

> *anticipates as good or better days to come, are to be found two chief ingredients of happiness …*
>
> *The months of our sojourning have hurried by too quickly …*
>
> *To every one upon this earth death cometh soon or late; but before it comes it is given to some to reach old age, not it may be the least pleasant period of life, but depending for much of its contentment on simple joys. And among these not the least may be reckoned the love of a garden, a pride and pleasure in the successful growth of the trees and shrubs and flowers you have planted yourself, in the smiling plenty of the wilderness you have tamed.*

We can only imagine the thoughts accompanying these sentiments as the view of the island disappeared into a blue haze, as his return journey to England began. Would he have looked back? I'm sure he would have been compelled to do so. In those last few precious moments, that image of the island's silhouette would have been ingrained into his memory once more, and as it finally faded, so too the process of preparing to adjust to life back in England would have begun.

*

Today's departures by sea have a definite air of dignity about them. A cruise ship's farewell to Funchal is in total contrast to its usually low-key, early-morning arrival. They have the habit of slipping into port with all the stealth of a night thief, with not so much as a whisper. One tends to wake from slumber to discover that the town's waterfront 'furnishings' have been rearranged, with the day's new arrivals already making themselves at home.

Departure, on the other hand, is a much grander, more ostentatious affair, conducted with a degree of high pomp. About an hour or so before departure, a thin wispy plume of smoke can be seen snaking its way from the ship's stack, a sure sign to any late-returning passengers of the need to make haste.

As the time for imminent departure approaches, three blasts from the ship's horn announce all is in readiness. Like Black Rod's knock on the House of Commons door, they are never in quick succession, but drawn out and unhurried. The remaining mooring lines are brought aboard, not by a heaving team of perspiring jacktars, but to the accompaniment of the electric whirr of the windlass, watched over by clean, well-suited deckhands and an officer.

A sort of lull then follows, with all eyes watching ship and quay, trying to spot the first signs of the ship's movement under her own steam. Ruffled waters at stem and stern suggest the thrusters have been engaged, pushing the hull gently away from the quay. Shoreside linesmen, having cast away the moorings which once held her steady and secure, watch as the distance between them turns into a gulf.

Passengers will, almost certainly, have gathered at the ship's rail, as if drawn there by magnetic pull. They play no part in the process of departure, but somehow they feel compelled to be there, to witness events first hand. It's a little like an act of remembrance; adherence is almost compulsory as the last rites of passage are performed. Perhaps it's also an innate reaction to leaving dry land once more. Although the passengers may have trod the Madeiran streets for only a few hours, the feel of firm soil is enough to remind them that we humans live on land, not water. Another forced temporary separation from our usual habitat just seems to tug at the natural psyche somewhere deep within.

The imagined forward movement of the liner then becomes a discernible reality, as she slowly glides towards the port entrance with all the nobility and pace befitting a ceremonial occasion, never rushed, everything in complete and utter control. At the front of this weighty procession, a small tug or pilot boat leads the advance, the Lord Lieutenant in this nautical pageant.

Even when the port entrance has been reached, there is never a sudden increase in speed. There's no suggestion that with the confines of the port passed, the engine crew are told to let the ship's hair down. In fact, another pause usually follows, to release a tow line or allow the pilot to disembark. The cortege gathers itself once more, and when all is ready, with grace and ease, the party moves slowly and silently on its way. Even a mile or more from the port, she seems to be steaming at just the same stately pace, perhaps unobtrusively gathering speed, but with any variation hardly discernible from the shore.

Departures at night have the added attraction of providing a unique light show. The subdued warm flicker of the dinner table candles contrast with the flashing multicoloured dazzling lights of the disco, and the ship's silhouette is etched by the white fluorescent deck light clusters. There is frequently more illumination on show on the average cruise ship than you would expect to find in a small village, spread not over a hillside but confined into a much smaller space, resembling a far-off floating funfair. Depending on the direction of the wind, wafts of music also occasionally cross the divide between us.

This image holds for some time, and as the ship fades towards the horizon, the lights seem to merge together before finally disappearing. And so, another consignment of tourists departs, a tribute to man's ability to pack up home and carry it with him, in pursuit of a more nomadic lifestyle. A self-contained world, oblivious to the everyday cares of the countries and communities it passes; until, that is, it reaches some other port, when for a few hours, their two worlds will combine.

*

For others not departing by sea, there is the drudgery of getting to the airport. Departure is a process which must be endured, and in this, the sea adieu has the upper hand. Barely has one entered the confines of the departure gate, having entrusted the luggage to the custody of a waiting airline attendant, than the island begins to relinquish its hold on you. Everything is still there, just beyond the windows. Sea, mountains, Desertas Islands, they are all in view, but it's as if, once inside the airport, the island is already a fading memory. By the time the aircraft wheels lift off from the tarmac, we are almost in 'home' mode, alert to face all that awaits the returning traveller.

For a day or so, you remain somehow mentally in touch with the island. Memories are never too far under the surface and can be reawakened in an instant. Then a few days will pass, and normality nudges them a little further from our reach. We begin to lose track of how long it was since we were there. Only four weeks ago? It seems longer. Time passes, memories fade, but for those who will come back next year, with each passing day the moment of return also shortens, until it becomes reality.

*

As for our own departure, the final hours are usually spent sitting in the early evening sunshine, beside the Capela de Santa Catarina in Santa Catarina Park. Overlooking a sun-soaked bay, feasting on the view from this slightly elevated position, our thoughts inevitably reflecting on the past twelve weeks.

Dark clouds sit on the mountaintop, like an old collier's cap pulled well down over a weathered forehead. The clouds are of little concern to us. The dying rays of the setting sun come from cloudless western skies. It's still warm, and the east of Funchal basks in an almost unnatural golden syrupy light, the sort photographers go to sleep and dream about.

Half a dozen or so single scull canoeists take exercise and paddle the waters around the lone cruiser, whose passengers are returning in time for their evening meal and another shared moment of departure. The *Santa Maria* rounds the harbour entrance after her pursuits in deep waters, her wooden hull creaking under the effort. Soon she'll be ready to tie up for the night.

I don't think there can be many better spots from which to watch the ending of any day. Time just slips idly by. Half an hour turns into an hour or more. We have little desire to stir. The sun still holds warmth, although from its duties here, it will soon be released.

We sit, not too far away from the quinta owned by C. T.-S. What we see is what he would undoubtedly have looked out upon a hundred years ago.

> *Here with jest and laughter we beguile the midday hours –*
>
> *"Light flows our war of mocking words;"*
>
> *and, when the sun declines, watch as we have often watched in wonder and delight before, the ravines of the opposite hills grow dark and mysterious in their evening haze, a foil for the heightened glow on peak and ridge.*

Tomorrow's weather promises much the same as today. A new band of pleasure-seekers will have slipped into port in the early hours; the park attendants will have tidied the gardens and swept the paths; the cafés and restaurants will have replenished stocks; and with everything returned to its best, a new cycle is ready to begin. As we prepare to leave, we too hold that image of the pretty bay, bathed in warm sunlight, firm in our minds, until we too return as we undoubtedly will.

But we leave the final words to the author. Someone who inspired this writing; someone with more than a transient passing interest in Madeira; someone who found the island had slowly seeped deep into his veins, becoming as much a part of him as the blood which coursed through them.

For C. T.-S. knew a return would never be too far away.

> *From faery lands forlorn we take ship upon perilous seas. We leave our garden and our well-beloved island at their best; never has spring smiled a sunnier smile; never has a garden been more prodigal of colour and perfume. In the turmoil of the busier life to which we are returning, we shall surely keep their memory green.*

It was always *au revoir*, never goodbye, and on each occasion he could have reminded himself of the words of poetry he had quoted, likening his departure to the *"The 'little death' of parting"*, for certain to be followed by *"The rapture of return"*.